vjbnf   S0-BBS-229
947.52 BELIA

Beliaev, Edward, author
Dagestan
33410015683594   02-01-2021

DISCARD

Valparaiso Public Library
103 Jefferson Street
Valparaiso, IN 46383

CULTURES OF THE WORLD
Dagestan

Cavendish
Square

New York

Published in 2021 by Cavendish Square Publishing, LLC
243 5th Avenue, Suite 136, New York, NY 10016
Copyright © 2021 by Cavendish Square Publishing, LLC

Third Edition

No part of this publication may be reproduced, stored in a retrieval system, or transmitted in any form or by any means—electronic, mechanical, photocopying, recording, or otherwise—without the prior permission of the copyright owner. Request for permission should be addressed to Permissions, Cavendish Square Publishing, 243 5th Avenue, Suite 136, New York, NY 10016. Tel (877) 980-4450; fax (877) 980-4454.

Website: cavendishsq.com

This publication represents the opinions and views of the author based on his or her personal experience, knowledge, and research. The information in this book serves as a general guide only. The author and publisher have used their best efforts in preparing this book and disclaim liability rising directly or indirectly from the use and application of this book.

All websites were available and accurate when this book was sent to press.

Cataloging-in-Publication Data

Names: Beliaev, Edward. | Buranbaeva, Oksana. | Morlock, Rachael.
Title: Dagestan / Edward Beliaev, Oksana Buranbaeva, and Rachael Morlock.
Description: New York : Cavendish Square, 2021. | Series: Cultures of the world
Identifiers: ISBN 9781502658807 (library bound) | ISBN 9781502658814 (ebook)
Subjects: LCSH: Dagestan (Russia)--Juvenile literature. | Dagestan (Russia)--Description and travel. | Dagestan (Russia)--History--Juvenile literature. | Dagestan (Russia)--Social life and customs.
Classification: LCC DK511.D2 B454 2021 | DDC 947.5'2--dc23

Writers, third edition: Edward Beliaev, Oksana Buranbaeva, Rachael Morlock
Editor, third edition: Rachael Morlock
Designer, third edition: Jessica Nevins
Picture Researcher, third edition: Jessica Nevins

Acknowledgments:
Edward Beliaev and Oksana Buranbaeva wish to thank Rimma Buranbaeva for her research assistance.

PICTURE CREDITS
The photographs in this book are used by permission and through the courtesy of: Cover Cholpan/Shutterstock.com; p. 1 Killovolt/iStock/Getty Images Plus; pp. 3, 13, 14 Suleyman Nabiev/EyeEm/Getty Images; p. 5 vostokphotos.ru/Moment/Getty Images; pp. 6, 37, 40, 51, 66, 114, 121 Musa Salgereyev\TASS via Getty Images; pp. 7, 76, 108 Yelena Afonina\TASS via Getty Images; pp. 9, 122 De Agostini Picture Library/Getty Images Plus; pp. 10, 54, 74 Hermes Images/ AGF/Universal Images Group via Getty Images; p. 12 Aleksey Petrov/500px/Getty Images; p. 16 Parshina Olga/iStock/Getty Images Plus; p. 18 Imagno/Getty Images; pp. 21, 80, 99, 109 Elena Odareeva/iStock/Getty Images Plus; p. 23 Interim Archives/Getty Images; p. 27 Fine Art Images/Heritage Images/Getty Images; p. 28 Aleksey Kivshenko/Wikimedia Commons/File:Imam Shamil surrendered to Count Baryatinsky on August 25, 1859 by Kivshenko, Alexei Danilovich.jpg/ CC-PD-Mark; p. 32 Antoine Gyori/Sygma via Getty Images; p. 34 Leonid Andronov/iStock/Getty Images Plus; pp. 38, 45, 46, 62, 69, 106 Vladimir Smirnov\ TASS via Getty Images; p. 39 Alexei Druzhinin\TASS via Getty Images; pp. 42, 83 undefined undefined/iStock/Getty Images Plus; p. 48 Vladimir Zapletin/ iStock/Getty Images Plus; p. 52 Mikushin/iStock/Getty Images Plus; p. 55 Reza/Getty Images; p. 56 Sergey Mayorov/500px Plus/Getty Images; p. 58 AlexStepanov/iStock Editorial/Getty Images Plus; p. 73 Bolshakov from Moscow, Russia/Wikimedia Commons/File:2011 wedding Makhachkala Dagestan 5532384898.jpg/CC-2.0; p. 78 Oleg Nikishin/Epsilon/Getty Images; pp. 84, 86 Alexander Demianchuk\TASS via Getty Images; p. 92 Scott Peterson/Getty Images; pp. 94, 116 Shamil Makhsumov/iStock/Getty Images Plus; p. 95 Sergei Rasulov\TASS via Getty Images; pp. 96, 111 Nikolay Korzhov/AFP via Getty Images; p. 97 Ali Atmaca/Anadolu Agency/Getty Images; pp. 100, 119, 130 Oskanov/iStock/Getty Images Plus; p. 103 Astrid Riecken for The Washington Post via Getty Images; p. 104 AbuUbayda/Wikimedia Commons/File:Avar theatre in Makhachkala.jpg/CC BY-SA (https://creativecommons.org/licenses/by-sa/3.0); p. 112 Stanislav Krasilnikov\TASS via Getty Images; p. 113 Jeff Bottari/Zuffa LLC/Zuffa LLC via Getty Images; p. 126 Radist/iStock/Getty Images Plus; p. 131 Yolya/iStock/Getty Images Plus; p. 137 alessandro0770/iStock/Getty Images Plus.

Some of the images in this book illustrate individuals who are models. The depictions do not imply actual situations or events.

CPSIA compliance information: Batch #CW21CSQ: For further information contact Cavendish Square Publishing LLC, New York, New York, at 1-877-980-4450.

Printed in the United States of America

Find us on

CONTENTS

DAGESTAN TODAY

WITH MUCH OF ITS LAND SANDWICHED BETWEEN MOUNTAINS and sea, the Republic of Dagestan is a beautiful but imposing place. Dagestan's harsh landscape has had a powerful impact on the course of the republic's history and the people who live there. A long parade of conquerors and invaders have entered Dagestan seeking land, resources, and access to the countries beyond its borders. That line of invaders began with the Persians in the sixth century and ended with the Russians in the 19th century. Today, Dagestan represents the southernmost reaches of the Russian Federation.

LAND OF MOUNTAINS

Over half of Dagestan is made up of rugged, mountainous terrain. It is difficult to cross, even with modern paved roads and well-equipped vehicles. The mountains rising throughout the southern half of Dagestan belong to the Greater Caucasus mountain range. In their upper reaches, mountain glaciers feed the region's mighty

Dagestan's landscape is a study in contrasts—from snow-covered peaks to blooming valleys and from rushing rivers to rolling sand dunes. The Andysky-Salatau mountain range is pictured here.

waterways. An extensive system of rivers carve through breathtaking gorges and canyons before emptying into the Caspian Sea.

For centuries, Dagestanis have creatively navigated the mountainous terrain. Early indigenous groups relied chiefly on raising livestock like sheep, goats, and cattle. Shepherds made seasonal migrations with their herds. They lived on the mountainsides in the spring and summer and traveled to lower pastures as colder temperatures set in. A system of using distant, seasonal pastures is still in practice for those who raise livestock in Dagestan today. Ancient peoples with access to Dagestan's limited arable land used terrace farming to make the most of the challenging environment. This strategy, along with extensive irrigation systems, is also a major part of the agricultural industry in modern Dagestan.

SEAWAYS AND THOROUGHFARES

The current republics of the North Caucasus region, including Dagestan, have a dynamic history of shared allegiances, struggles for independence, and indigenous ethnicities. They have been the subject of repeated wars. Empires in search of trading routes, radicals fighting holy wars, rulers looking to expand their domain, and soldiers seeking military advantages all pursued their own agendas against the backdrop of the North Caucasus region.

Dagestan was particularly desired by outsiders because of its strategic location. The port city of Derbent in southern Dagestan, one of the oldest cities in Russia, was the gateway to the Caucasus. Positioned on the coast of the Caspian Sea near a critical mountain pass, Derbent was an important stop along the Silk Road trade route. Travelers, merchants, and armies crossing between Europe and the Middle East passed through Derbent. The city was besieged by Caucasian Albanians, Persians, Khazars, Arabs, Seljuk Turks, Azeris, Mongols, and the Russian Empire at various points in its long timeline.

The Caspian Sea forms Dagestan's eastern border. This important natural landmark makes sea routes for trade and transportation possible between Dagestan and its neighbors.

For Dagestanis, the Caspian coastline continues to be an important center of collective history, cultural exchange, and natural resources. Two of Dagestan's most important modern cities, Derbent and Makhachkala, are situated on its shores. The Caspian Sea offers plentiful economic resources for Dagestan, with its rich oil and natural gas reserves, critical habitat for native species, and popular seaside tourist attractions.

MANY ETHNICITIES

Dagestan is remarkable for its range of cultures and languages as a multinational republic. It is the most ethnically diverse entity in the Russian Federation. Members of more than 30 indigenous ethnic groups and 110 nationalities live in Dagestan. The republic has 14 official languages belonging to the 14 most populous ethnic groups in the area. The five largest ethnic groups are Avars, Dargins, Kumyks, Lezgins, and Laks.

Indigenous peoples, their unique cultural and religious traditions, and their interaction with outside powers have created a deep legacy in Dagestan. Five locations in Derbent are designated as UNESCO World Heritage Sites because of their historic and cultural importance. These include the ancient wall of Derbent, the Derbent Lighthouse, the Juma Mosque, Naryn-Kala in the Derbent Fortress, and the Armenian Church of the Holy Savior.

The artisan crafts of many indigenous groups are also distinctive hallmarks of Dagestani culture. Handwoven carpets from southern Dagestan are known around the world for their exquisite artistry. Goldsmiths, silversmiths, potters, woodworkers, and weavers have strong ties to the ethnic communities that have sustained a legacy of excellence in each field for centuries.

SEEKING STABILITY

Only a small portion of Dagestan's population survives in the highlands today, but the majority of people still live outside of the republic's major cities. Raising livestock, growing crops, and other agricultural activities employ a large portion of Dagestan's workforce. However, the area continues to suffer from economic setbacks, unemployment, and poverty. Dagestan is one of the poorest republics in Russia.

A turbulent history of invasion and political struggle, from ancient times to the more recent Chechen Wars, have led to poverty, corruption, and conflict in Dagestan. Ongoing violence related to ethnic and religious tensions have given Dagestan an international reputation as a dangerous place to live and visit. Violence reached new levels after the Second Chechen War. Then, religious extremism plagued the republic as fundamentalist Islamic factions gained support in the region. Dagestan also made international headlines in 2013 when ties between the Boston Marathon bombing in the United States and Dagestan came to light.

The tiered layout of Gimry village shows how Dagestanis have adapted their settlements to the mountainous terrain of the region.

Although religious radicals have harmed the republic, Dagestan's identity as a majority-Muslim republic has helped it to weather social and political changes. With more than 90 percent of the population sharing a common bond of religion, attitudes toward ethnic and cultural differences are more open. Dagestan may be perceived by some as a dangerous land, but it also has a reputation for exceptional hospitality. Travelers to the remote region draw attention, and they are often warmly welcomed with feasts and a glimpse into the cultural ways that have persevered throughout Dagestan's long history.

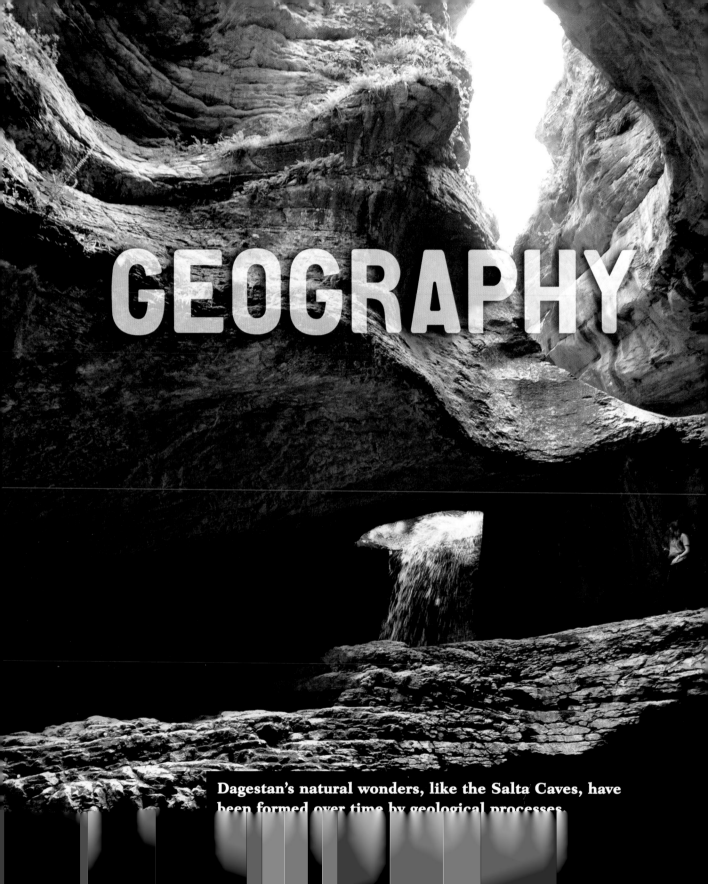

GEOGRAPHY

Dagestan's natural wonders, like the Salta Caves, have been formed over time by geological processes.

1

FOR A RELATIVELY SMALL REPUBLIC, Dagestan's geography is composed of a variety of terrains. Its area measures about 19,400 square miles (50,300 square kilometers). Mountains, foothills, high-altitude plateaus, and lowlands mark the landscape. Perhaps best known for the Caucasus mountain range, which crosses its southern and central regions, Dagestan also hosts 336 miles (540 km) of coast along the Caspian Sea. More than 1,800 rivers cross the republic. Aside from its eastern seaside border, Dagestan is flanked by several Russian entities. The Republic of Kalmykia lies to the north on the other side of the Kuma River. Dagestan shares its western borders with the Stavropol Territory and Chechnya. International borders with Georgia and Azerbaijan lie in the mountainous south.

Dagestan's total land area is slightly smaller than the country of Costa Rica and roughly twice the size of the U.S. state of Vermont.

MOUNTAINS AND FOOTHILLS

The Caucasus Mountains stretch northwest to southeast between the Black Sea and the Caspian Sea. They are made up of two main ranges, the Greater Caucasus to the north and the Lesser Caucasus to the south. The watershed of the Greater Caucasus is a large swath of land that forms a boundary between Europe and Central Asia.

The Greater Caucasus travel through the southern half of Dagestan, where they reach their greatest width. The main crest ridge of the Greater Caucasus forms Dagestan's southern border. This is where the region's highest points can be found. Mount Bazardyuzyu (also known as Bazardyuze Dagi), located on the border with Azerbaijan, boasts the highest peak at 14,652 feet (4,466 m). Other impressive summits along this ridge are Addala Shukhgelmezr at 13,622 feet (4,152 m) and Dyul'tydag at 13,540 feet (4,127 m).

From the watershed ridge near Dagestan's southern border, the mountainous terrain stretches to the north. This area contains a large triangle of mountain ranges known as the Dagestan Interior Highland. The Gimrinsky and Andysky-Salatau ranges there are characterized by

The famous Sulak Canyon draws crowds with its natural beauty. The canyon is about 33 miles (53 km) long and is navigated by the turquoise Sulak River.

high crests, deep valleys, and stunning canyons. The Sulak, Samur, and Kurakh rivers flow through the Interior Highland toward the Caspian Sea. Along the Sulak Canyon, the highest point towers 6,299 feet (1,920 m) above the river. It is the deepest canyon in Russia.

A zone of foreland hills is located north of the Caucasus and the Dagestan Interior Highland. The width of this zone fluctuates between 12 and 25 miles (19 and 40 km). Foothills in this area can reach up to 3,000 feet (914 m) high.

CASPIAN COAST AND LOWLANDS

A narrow strip of land is squeezed between Dagestan's mountains and the Caspian Sea in the southeast. This coastal plain is only 2 miles (3 km) wide in some places, but it broadens out to 20 miles (32 km) in others. Rivers pass through the area on their way to the sea, leaving behind rich sedimentary deposits.

The coastal plain is where two of Dagestan's largest cities are located. Derbent is an ancient city built along the Caspian shore in southern Dagestan. Makhachkala, Dagestan's capital, is situated about 79 miles (128 km) to the north along the thin coastal strip.

Dagestan's Caspian coastline stretches for 336 miles (540 km). The sandy beaches and warm waters draw residents and visitors alike for vacationing or for therapeutic treatments at spas. However, there is a shortage of freshwater through most of the area.

The Caspian lowlands continue northward. Farmers and herders move their livestock from the mountains to these low-lying pastures in winter. A considerable part of the lowlands lies below the level of the Caspian Sea. Agriculture flourishes in the region. In contrast, the Nogay Steppe is a hot and dry area between the Terek and Kuma Rivers. This northern steppe is not friendly to much vegetation besides sagebrush.

Major cities in Dagestan include Makhachkala, Kaspiysk, Derbent, Kizlyar, Izberbash, and Buynaksk.

Kaspiysk, located along the Caspian Sea, is one of the largest cities in Dagestan.

Makhachkala is the capital of Dagestan. The city is located in the coastal plain along the Caspian Sea. Originally part of Kumyk territory, the area captured the attention of Persians, Huns, Arabs, and Russians seeking a route through the Caucasus Mountains. In 1844, a Russian military fortress was founded where the city now stands. It was named Petrovskoye after Czar Peter the Great. Makhachkala evolved into a seaport and center of trade and was named Petrovsk Port in 1857. After the city became Dagestan's capital in 1921, it was renamed for a Dagestani revolutionary known as Makhach.

Today, Makhachkala is home to more than half a million residents with diverse ethnic backgrounds. The city maintains trade and transportation routes between Dagestan and its neighbors by air, sea, and rail. It is the base for many governmental, cultural, religious, and educational institutions in Dagestan and one of the largest cities in the North Caucasus.

Makhachkala brings together some of Dagestan's finest features—the foothills of the Caucasus, the expansive Caspian Sea, and the rich coexistence of multiethnic populations.

Two prominent bays mark the coast. Kizlyarski Bay is located where the Kuma River flows into the Caspian Sea. Agrahanski Bay lies between the Terek River delta and the sandy Agrakhan Peninsula. There are several islands along the Caspian coast that belong to Dagestan. The islands Chechen and Tyuleniy are among the largest.

RIVERS

The Kuma River serves as a border between Dagestan and Kalmykiya. It flows northeast and empties into the Caspian Sea. It usually dries up by midsummer because of irrigation canals that drain much of its water. In the extensive Kuma delta region, marshes cover much of the area.

The Terek River, probably the best known of the Caucasus rivers, unrolls for 370 miles (600 km). The Terek formed the southern border of the Russian settlement in the Caucasus until the 1860s. It begins in the glaciers of the Caucasus in northern Georgia. From there, it flows through high mountain terrain and gorges to the foothills and plains of Ingushetiya, Chechnya, and Dagestan. The river's lower courses are used to irrigate farmland. South of the city of Kizlyar, the swampy delta of the Terek is about 60 miles (100 km) wide.

The Sulak and the Samur are two other major rivers that flow from the Caucasus Mountains to the Caspian Sea, traveling through gorges and canyons. Dagestan's system of rivers is quite extensive. The Sulak, for example, is a grouping of rivers unto itself. It consists of the main channel of the Sulak as well as the Avarskoye Koysu, Andiyskoye Koysu, Kazikumukhskoye Koysu, and Kara Koysu.

Dagestan's rivers are not navigable for large vessels. Most flood during the spring when snow and ice in the Caucasus melt. They are used for hydroelectric power, as a water supply, and for transporting logs produced by the timber industry. Hydroelectric power plants are located at Gergebil along the Kara Koysu; at Chirkey, Chiryurt, and Kizilyurt on the Sulak River; and at Kargalinskaya on the Terek River. Small lakes are found mostly in the lower reaches of the Terek and Sulak.

CLIMATE AND RESOURCES

Dagestan's climate is generally mild and dry. Naturally, conditions vary considerably with the terrain. Dagestan's average January temperature is 36 degrees Fahrenheit (2.2 degrees Celsius), and its average July temperature is 72°F (22.2°C). Lowland temperatures are usually higher, while mountain temperatures tend to be lower.

Just as temperatures change, annual precipitation also varies from the lowlands to the mountains. In general, the least rainfall occurs in the Nogay Steppe. This sandy landscape receives only 8 to 10 inches (200 to 250 millimeters) of rainfall a year. The most rainfall is recorded in the

"Térek bellows, wildly sweeping
Past the cliffs, so swift and strong;
Like a tempest is his weeping,
Flies his spray like tears along.
O'er the steppe now slowly veering—
Calm but faithless looketh he—
With a voice of love endearing
Murmurs to the Caspian sea:"
    —From "The Gift of the Terek" by Mikhail Lermontov

zone of foreland hills. Unlike the dry mountainous regions to the south, this zone averages 20 to 30 inches (510 to 760 mm) of rainfall each year.

The soil also varies with the terrain. In the Nogay Steppe, the soil is not suited for agriculture. However, in the foothills, a much richer, blacker soil is found. As a result, a variety of grasses and vegetation thrives there. In the higher foothills where precipitation is greatest, there are forests of oak, beech, hornbeam, maple, poplar, and black alder. In the mountains, birches and pines grow, as well as the tough, adaptable plants and low trees that live in the alpine meadows.

Valuable resources are found in the rich reserves of oil and gas beneath the Caspian Sea, only some of which are in Dagestani territory. These valuable substances have given rise to oil refineries and the chemical industry. Mineral resources are hidden in Dagestan's many mountain chains, but they are generally difficult and costly to extract due to the harsh terrain and climate.

WILDLIFE

The variations in climate have produced differences in the plant and animal life across Dagestan. Dagestan's native wildlife includes 89 species of mammals, 300 bird species, and 92 species of fish. Mammals such as bears, wolves, foxes, badgers, Eurasian lynx, chamois, roe deer, wild boar, and hares live in

The Sarykum Sand Dune rises out of an arid territory not far from Makhachkala. It is the largest sand dune in Eurasia.

the mountainous terrain. Goats, like the bezoar goat and Dagestani tur, can live at high elevations, scrambling up steep mountainsides. Leopards are also native to the region, though it is difficult to estimate how many remain in the Caucasus Mountains of Dagestan.

The Dagestan Nature Reserve protects native habitats in several locations around the republic. One area encompasses the Sarykum Sand Dune, an 860-foot (262 m) dune and part of an ecosystem with native plants, birds, insects, and snakes. Temperatures at the dune have been recorded to reach 108°F (42.2°C). In the Kizlyarski Bay region, wildlife sanctuaries protect marshy wetlands, native grasses, and a wide variety of waterfowl and migratory birds.

INTERNET LINKS

https://www.britannica.com/place/Caucasus
Find a thorough overview of the Caucasus Mountains in Dagestan and beyond in this article.

http://dagzapoved.ru/
This website for the Dagestan Reserve includes information about the animals, plants, and ecosystems under its protection.

http://www.wild-russia.org/bioregion3/Dagestansky/3_dagest.htm
The Center for Russian Nature Conservation offers this web page with images and facts about the biodiversity of Dagestan's natural reserves.

HISTORY

Dagestan's location has made it an enviable territory for conquering armies throughout history. When this photo was taken in Gunib in 1890, Dagestan was under the control of Imperial Russia.

2

DAGESTAN'S NAME GIVES CLUES TO the long history of invasion and conquest that has shaped its character. *Dag* is a Turkish word for "mountain," while —*stan* is a Persian suffix meaning "land of." In addition to the Persians and Ottoman Turks who vied for control in the lands of today's Dagestan, the region was also sought by Romans, Mongolians, Arabs, Timurs, and Russians. Land passed back and forth between various groups for much of the republic's 3,000-year history. It was not until 1921 that Dagestan as we know it today emerged from the various battlefields of history. At that time, Soviet authorities drew state boundaries, and the Dagestan Autonomous Soviet Socialist Republic was established as part of the new Soviet Union.

In 1919, parts of Dagestan and Chechnya formed the North Caucasus Emirate in a push for religious and political independence.

Before that time, the territory that would become known as Dagestan never had precise or set borders. It was populated by different tribes, some of which spoke similar languages, while others had their own dialects and languages. Over many centuries, a wide range of peoples migrated in and out of the territory.

Because the Caucasus as a whole is a relatively small and contained region—when compared to the rest of Russia or stretches of Central Asia—the groups that settled there have been closely interacting for centuries. Organized states have existed in the region since the end of the first millennium CE. They would emerge, then collapse, and then new states would appear to replace them, often in the form of loose confederations of peoples, clans, and tribes.

Thus, the history of present-day Dagestan includes the history of the entire Caucasus region. Dagestan's ever-changing borders and its inhabitants have been influenced by forces originating both within and beyond the republic. Even today, Dagestan maintains close, if sometimes tense, relationships with its neighbors in the Caucasus. Many ethnic and religious groups share ties across state and international boundaries that forge strong and dynamic bonds.

THE ANCIENT CAUCASUS

Archaeologists have concluded that the territory that makes up present-day Dagestan has been continuously inhabited since the Stone Age. A narrow strip along the Caspian Sea—about 2 miles (3 km) wide near the city of Derbent, between the sea and the high mountains—served from ancient times as a migration route for many peoples. It was also an access point for a series of foreign invaders. Derbent, which was eventually founded in 438 CE as a Persian fortress, guarded the important caravan route that stretched from southwestern Europe to southwestern Asia. Because this key avenue for trade passed through Dagestani territory, the area became the home of a diverse range of peoples and cultures.

The Caucasus also became one of the major routes along which technological innovations spread from Asia and the Middle East to Europe. Significant strides in the development of metallurgy were made in the Caucasus. These innovations then spread to the outlying regions. Metalworkers initially focused on copper,

The area around Derbent has been an important settlement in Dagestan since at least the eighth century BCE. Derbent itself is said to be the oldest city in Russia. It is also Russia's most southern city.

Construction on Derbent's citadel began in 570 CE, and the same structure has been largely maintained since then. Two parallel walls were built to span 2.2 miles (3.5 km) from the mountains directly to the Caspian Sea. The walls are up to 10.5 feet (3.2 m) thick and 49 feet (15 m) high. The northern wall still stands today, but the southern wall was destroyed in the 19th century.

Derbent's ancient history and importance to the Silk Road have earned its designation as a **UNESCO** World Heritage Site. The walls of the **Naryn-Kala Citadel** can be seen here.

The city, citadel, and walls cover about 25 acres (10 hectares) of land. This historic area contains ancient gates, defense towers, an eighth-century mosque, a bathhouse, and the winding streets of a city that continues to defend its importance on the world map.

then later turned their attention to bronze and iron. This progression is not surprising, as the Caucasus are rich in metal ores.

Early in the region's history, several tribes, including the Legues, Guels, and Utines, formed alliances. At the end of the first millennium BCE, some of these groupings united to form a large state—called Caucasian Albania—in the eastern Caucasus. Around that time, a few cities emerged in Dagestani territory, including Chola, Toprakhkala, and Urtseki.

When the Mongols invaded Dagestan in the 14th century, they were met with the highland's most ferocious fighters. Partu Patimat was an unlikely hero of the period. Retellings of her story have inspired countless generations of Dagestanis.

Timur, also called Tamerlane, was a Mongol warrior who invaded Dagestan. He looted and raided the region before passing near the village of a young woman named Partu Patimat. According to the legends and ballads created about her, Patimat led her community into battle against Timur and his army in 1396. Patimat is often described as a lion, and the image of the young woman victoriously riding her horse into battle has drawn comparisons to France's Joan of Arc. Patimat has come to symbolize the strength, resilience, and determination of Dagestan's mountain dwellers. Many Dagestani girls are still named Patima or Patimat in her honor.

EMPIRES AND INVASIONS

In the third century CE, the Sassanids from Persia invaded the southern part of present-day Dagestan, making it all the way to the contemporary city of Derbent. A century later, the Huns captured the coastline to the north of Derbent. By the fourth century, sizable cities had emerged on the coast. Derbent, Semender, and Zerekhgeran (Kubachi) became increasingly large and bustling urban centers. Handicrafts and a sizable trade network also began to develop in the region.

In the seventh century, Dagestan became the target of repeated invasions by the Arabs, who tried to convert the tribes to Islam. The people resisted, sometimes with the help of their northern neighbor, the Khazar Khanate. (A khanate was a political group or state led by a ruler called a khan.) In exchange, the people would assist other regions beset by Arab invaders. In 851, fighters supported a Georgian revolt against the Arabs. Then, in 905 and also from 913 to 914, the united tribes defeated the Arab-controlled vassals in Shirvan and Derbent. The Arabs, however, left a lasting mark on the region's native residents. The Arabs not only converted them to Islam, sometimes forcibly, they also introduced their writings and handicrafts to the area.

In the middle of the 11th century, the Seljuks captured the territory that now includes Azerbaijan and a considerable part of Dagestan. A century later, several independent states emerged in Dagestan, including the Avar Khanate, Kazikumukh Shamkhal, Utsmi of Kaitag, and other small political groupings. Repeated attempts made by these confederations to unite all of Dagestan under their rule failed. Wars and ethnic conflicts prevented the goal from being realized.

As in the past, the region became subject to continued waves of invasion. In the 1220s, Dagestan was exposed to the overwhelming onslaught of the Mongols. Then, in the 14th century, the Uzbek, Tokhtamysh, and Timur armies invaded the region.

This 17th-century view of Fort Terki accompanied a book by Adam Olearius called *Very Unusual Travels in Muscovy, Tartary, and Persia*. Olearius visited the region from Germany to study possible Persian trade routes.

In the 16th century, especially after the Muscovite state annexed the Kazan (1552) and Astrakhan (1556) Khanates, the Russians extended their area of control and influence that much closer to the territory that would become the Republic of Dagestan. As a result, ties between Moscow and the people living in the region became more entwined. The Russians, to defend their southern frontier from the Ottomans and other Turkic tribes, established forts along the Terek River. The most prominent was Fort Terki, founded by L. Novoseltsev of Astrakhan in 1577 at the confluence of the Sunzha and Terek Rivers. Then, in 1583, the fort was moved to the mouth of the Terek.

The forts served a military purpose, but they were also places of commercial exchange between the Russians and the mountain peoples. The tribes needed items such as grain, so they came to the plains to bargain for goods. They often exchanged sheep for grain or firearms. Cossacks had established themselves in the region by the first half of the 16th century. Cossacks were groups of peasants of Russian or Polish descent. By the end of the century, a large number of the Cossack frontiersmen lived along the Terek. The Russian government used the Cossacks to defend its southern border and paid them for their services with money, grains, firearms, and munitions.

Relations with the local tribes were often friendly. The Russian leaders and Cossacks formed fluid alliances with some of the tribes, helping them defend themselves from enemies. At other times, groups of opposing forces united and attacked the Russians. In this unstable political climate, some Dagestani rulers sought Russian protection. Thus, in the first half of the 17th century, the Shamkhal of Tarku, the Utsmi of Kaitag, and other peoples accepted and submitted to Russian suzerainty. This meant that Russia, the dominant foreign power, controlled the region's foreign relations but allowed the area's leaders to oversee local and internal affairs.

In 1722, weaknesses in the Persian Empire prompted Czar Peter the Great to invade the part of the eastern Caucasus controlled by the Persians. From the Volga River, Peter traveled south along the coast of the Caspian Sea to easily penetrate Persian-held territory. He was soon forced to withdraw, but as a result of this campaign, Russia gained control of the western coast of the Caspian Sea. However, in 1735, by the terms of the Ganjin Treaty with Persia, Russia removed its troops from the coast. Meanwhile, in the northern Caucasus, Russia started to build a network of military settlements and forged alliances with the princes of Kabardia. This part of the region was located close to the Black Sea coast and occupied by the Ottomans.

Through the entire 18th century, Russian leaders utilized the speed and force of the Cossacks. They actively engaged in colonizing and building a line of defense along the Terek River and farther to the west. New important fortress towns were built, among them Vladikavkas in 1784 (the present-day capital of North Ossetia) and Grozny in 1818 (the present-day capital of Chechnya).

In 1796, the Russians occupied the Caspian coast at Derbent and forced some local khanates and free tribes to submit to their rule. In 1813, according to the terms of the Gulistan Peace Treaty, Persia finally ceded control of those khanates along the Caspian Sea from Lenkoran (located in present-day Azerbaijan, near the border with Iran) to Derbent to Russia. It was at that point, for the first time, that all the geographic areas that make up present-day Dagestan were under Russian ownership.

RUSSIAN ADVANCES

The Russians had started to gain inroads into the region during the 16th century, mostly on the plains along the Terek and Kuban Rivers. Relations between the Russian settlers and local tribes were usually friendly and mutually beneficial. Therefore, in Dagestan in the beginning of the 19th century, several khanates and free communities accepted Russian suzerainty. The ruler of Avaria, the most important khanate in Dagestan, submitted to suzerainty in 1803. Avaria refers to the political structure of the Avar people, one of the largest groups in the area. They were mainly located in the mountainous regions of central and northwestern Dagestan.

By the middle of the 1820s, Dagestan appeared to be under the full control of Russia. Nevertheless, the 19th century witnessed a ferocious war in the northern Caucasus. Lasting from 1817 to 1864, it started soon after Russia annexed the southern Caucasus, or the area that makes up present-day Georgia, Azerbaijan, and Armenia.

The conflict arose for various reasons. Rulers in the northern and southern Caucasus were motivated to come under Russian protection by the constant threat of strife in the region between the great regional powers—most notably the Persians and Ottomans. Interregional wars were also continuously fought among the rulers themselves and their numerous factions. To add to the complex situation, some of the rulers who submitted to Russian control would later rebel against that strong central power. Often, Russia ruthlessly crushed rebel forces and annexed their territory.

When Russia became the sole power in most of the Caucasus in the beginning of the 19th century, the need to ensure safe communication lines between Russia and its newly annexed territories south of the Caucasus watershed ridge became essential. Russia felt it had to suppress unruly mountain tribes living in the northern Caucasus. These groups made frequent incursions on Russian forts and managed to disrupt communications. Economic, religious, and cultural factors also played an important role in this fight. General A. P. Yermolov, the Russian commander in the Caucasus, restlessly advanced through the mountainous regions of Chechnya and Dagestan and placed pressure on the local population. They were forced to either resettle in the flatlands under the protection of the watchful Russian garrisons or to move even farther and higher into the mountains.

Either way, this totally disrupted the way of life among the mountain people. The upheaval and lack of stability prompted some Dagestani rulers to unite against the Russians. During the first years of the uprising, they suffered nothing but defeat. The Russians then confiscated the rebels' lands or handed them over to vassals. The rebels attempted to enlist the support of the Persians and Ottomans against Russia, but it was too late. Russia had become too strong. From 1826 to 1828, Russia defeated Persia and seized control of the Yerevan and Nakhichevan Khanates (in present-day Armenia and Azerbaijan, respectively). Then, as a result of the 1828—1829 war with the Ottoman Empire, Russia acquired part of the Black Sea coast. The extent of its holding included the forts of Akhaltsikhe and Akhalkalaki in present-day Georgia, not far from the Turkish border.

The aggression and frequent cruelty of the Russian army toward the area's native residents often led to spontaneous mass rebellions. The first happened in Chechnya in 1825. It was suppressed the following year. Then, in the late 1820s, one of the most interesting phenomena of this period emerged. A religious movement called Muridism, which was basically a form of the branch of Islam called Sufism, arrived in the region.

In general, murid means "disciple." When applied to the Caucasus region, the term refers to a follower of a sheikh in the Islamic mystical tradition of Sufism. The Murids of the northeastern and north-central Caucasus (mostly Dagestan and Chechnya) in the 19th century were actually warriors set on expelling the Russian invaders.

The history of Muridism is often associated with the somewhat mysterious figure of Elisha Mansur. Some say that he was an Italian Dominican sent by the pope to convert the Greeks of Anatolia (an area of present-day Turkey that was controlled by the Ottoman Empire) to Catholicism. However, he converted to Islam and was subsequently sent by the sultan to organize the Caucasian resistance against the Russians. Others say that he was a Chechen. Either way, he was able to forge a broad ethnic coalition of Muslims until he was captured in 1795. Mansur is a legendary and heroic figure for the Chechens.

THE IMAMATE

The political aspect of Muridism was developed by Imam Muhammad, also known as Ghazi Muhammad or Ghazi Mullah. He was a Muslim leader who called for a holy war, or jihad, against the Russians. Ghazi Muhammad was the first of three imams (leaders) to create a theocratic, or religion-based, state called an imamate. It existed for almost three decades, from the early 1830s to 1859.

Ghazi Muhammad was a pupil of Mansur. He began his own preaching in 1827. The main thrust of his ministry was to encourage the Caucasian people to fully accept Islam. He urged them to replace their customary laws, which had divided them, with Muslim laws. He encouraged the community to stand united against the Russians. In 1829, he spread his message throughout Dagestan. Muslim scholars proclaimed him imam, or leader, and pledged their support of his armed struggle against the Russians and of his mission to strengthen Islam in the region.

Shamil was born in Dagestan in 1797. He is a founding figure in Dagestani history and is still honored as a hero.

Ghazi Muhammad was killed by the Russian army during a skirmish at the village of Gimry in 1832. Imam Gamzat-bek (also known as Hamza-bek) took his place. He was killed two years later by Avars who were formerly his supporters. The third imam was a close friend of Ghazi Muhammad named Shamil. Imam Shamil was able to draw support from the Murids as well as from the mountain peoples to create a quasi-state in the North Caucasus.

When Shamil became imam, the Russian forces were distracted in the western part of the northern Caucasus, where they were fighting the Circassians. Shamil took advantage of the situation to extend his influence over the tribes that had not made their loyalties known. Under Shamil's guidance, the imamate became larger, stronger, and better organized. When the Russians were again prepared to strike against the imamate, he was ready. The Russians

Shamil surrendered to Russian Count Baryatinsky in 1859. The site of the surrender has since been marked with a structure known as both Baryatinsky's Stone and the Gazebo of Shamil.

Hadji Murat was an Avar mountaineer who fought on both sides of the Caucasian War. The famous Russian writer Leo Tolstoy wrote and named a novel for him.

met with not only Shamil's formidable forces but also the extremely difficult terrain of the region.

In 1838, the Russians were able to capture the *aoul* (ah-OOL), or village, Akhoulgo, where Shamil was quartered with his people. However, Shamil escaped. He seemed to have been on the edge of defeat, but Circassians in the west reorganized and resumed their attacks on the Russian fortresses. This diversion gave Shamil time to regroup. The success of the Circassians in seizing a couple of Russian forts and military posts in the western Caucasus rekindled the rebellious spirit of the tribes living in the north-central Caucasus that had previously given up the fight. Shamil got the much-needed support of the Chechens. He then started harassing the Russian troops, often raiding several of their posts in a single day. The Russians were vulnerable to attack at any moment, and their expedition of 1839 almost had to abandon its campaign.

Shamil enjoyed the widespread support of the Caucasian population, who supplied him with men and horses. In the 1840s, Shamil had 25,000 cavalrymen at his disposal. The imamate occupied all of Chechnya, part of Dagestan, and parts of present-day Georgia and Azerbaijan. However, it did not succeed in some territories of Dagestan. The khan of the Avars and Shamkhal of Tarku, for example, who had leaned toward Russian support, refused to recognize the suzerainty of the imam.

In 1843, Shamil captured all of the Russian military posts in Avaria and blockaded the rest of the Russian forces that remained in Dagestan. An accomplished military strategist, he knew when to attack and when to wait until the Russians were exhausted and weakened by disease, cold weather, and the loss of men. He tried to forge an alliance with the Turks and the British during the Crimean War of 1853 to 1856, but neither group would side with him. However, due to his increased visibility in the region, he was widely known and admired in western Europe for his military genius and bravery.

Shamil waged a long and often successful war against the Russians. Within the imamate, he introduced laws, a postal system, taxes, and an ever-increasing roster of duties. Eventually, this strategy became the imamate's main problem. The lengthy war, strict discipline, heavy tax burden, and rigorous duties (including supplying men and horses to the Murids) exhausted the people and created opposition to the Muridist regime.

The Russians eventually prevailed. In 1857, a large, well-equipped Russian army started closing in on Shamil. In the face of such pressure, many tribes and villages surrendered. Finally, in 1859, isolated with his small group of followers, Shamil surrendered himself and was brought to Saint Petersburg.

Shamil's surrender marked the end of the imamate and the Murids. This conflict in the northern Caucasus is known as the Caucasian War. Though it was waged across the northern Caucasus and ended with the defeat of the Chechens in 1864, the most important fighting took place in Dagestan.

DEVELOPING DAGESTAN

After Shamil's surrender and the end of the imamate, the Dagestani region came fully under Russian control in 1860. Resistance to Russian rule continued for the rest of the century. Notable uprisings were organized jointly by Chechens and Dagestanis who were unhappy with the Russian suppression of Islam. These took place throughout the 1860s and 1870s and were met with ruthless reprisals from the Imperial Russian authorities. Often, insurgents were hanged or exiled. The seeds of Dagestani nationalism and anti-Russian sentiment were planted and developed against this backdrop.

The liberation of serfs and slaves had come to the Caucasus by the mid-1860s. Economic reform was not far behind. Although the reform was not comprehensive, such developments helped to spur commercial and industrial modernization in Dagestan. The construction of a railroad connecting Dagestan with the rest of Russia brought even greater changes. Various industrial enterprises continued to be built in the late 19th century, including oil refineries and food-processing centers. Huge farms were established in the flatlands and the foothills by Russian landlords and worked by the many Russian peasants urged to emigrate to the region.

Russians also brought their cultural practices with them. In some areas, tensions grew between indigenous Dagestanis and ethnic Russians. Many

Shamil was exiled to a mansion near Moscow and given an income by the czar. He died in 1871.

Russian intellectuals and academics got to work studying Dagestani geography, soils, climate, history, languages, and anthropology. All of this activity gradually led to the emergence of Dagestan's own intelligentsia, who played a considerable role in the pre- and post-revolutionary turmoil that would grip the northern Caucasus in the coming years.

Dagestan became a battleground once again when World War I broke out in 1914. The Russian Empire was broken and depleted by the war. In 1917, the czar abdicated in the face of a wide-scale revolution. Immediately after the Revolution of 1917 in Russia, Dagestan's intelligentsia, including the mullahs, or Muslim leaders, began to call for an independent Dagestan. They established the society Jamia al Islamia in April 1917.

A SOVIET REPUBLIC

After the Russian Revolution, chaos ruled in the entire Caucasus region, including Dagestan. The situation became worse when civil war erupted in Russia, which eventually led to the creation of the Soviet Union. Various groups in Dagestan rose up in renewed bids for independence. In the end, they lacked the unity necessary to make a lasting change in the face of the civil war's violence and unrest. As the war began to settle, Dagestan's leaders sought assurances that their local ethnic groups, cultures, and languages would be respected and protected under a new Soviet organization. In January 1921, the Soviet government in Moscow established the Dagestan Autonomous Soviet Socialist Republic within the framework of the Russian Soviet socialist republics.

Then, in December of that year, the Constituent Assembly of Dagestan adopted a constitution and governmental institutions based on the Soviet model. From 1921 to 1991, the newly created political entity had a parliament called the Supreme Soviet of the Dagestan Autonomous Soviet Socialist Republic.

Moscow had a heavy hand in the governing of the Caucasus, but Dagestan made new strides in economic and social development during the Soviet period. A modern oil industry, dozens of large- and middle-sized enterprises in a range of industries, and around 150 electric power plants were established. A more skilled workforce emerged during the period, in which agriculture became a more highly industrialized venture.

During World War II (1939—1945), the German army occupied some territory in the northern Caucasus but was stopped by the Soviet army at the Mosdok-Vladikavkas line. Thus, Dagestan avoided occupation by the Germans. Still, the enemy faction had advanced to within 100 miles (161 km) of the republic's border. During the war, several indigenous peoples of the Caucasus, including Dagestan's neighboring groups the Chechens and the Ingush, were deported to central Asia under the rule of Soviet leader Joseph Stalin. Dagestani peoples were spared this atrocity, but the upheaval sent shock waves through the entire Caucasus region. The forced exile served as a powerful reminder of the czarist wars against the native residents of the area.

Despite the period of industrialization under Stalin, Dagestan remained one of the least developed republics in the Soviet Union. Some economic improvements arrived in the area through reforms in the 1980s. Programs designed to spur productivity brought a much-needed boost to Dagestan. The loosening of Soviet attitudes by this time also allowed for a new commitment to Islam in Dagestan and a freer exploration of cultural identity.

AFTER THE SOVIETS

The beginning of the 1990s was another period of upheaval. The Soviet Union dissolved in 1991, and political, social, and cultural changes shook the northern Caucasus region. First, many autonomous republics wanted to become independent, sovereign nations. Then, there was a movement for the creation of a mountain republic, which would unite all the ethnic republics of the northern Caucasus. This was followed by a war in Chechnya, which started in 1994.

Now known as the First Chechen War, it led to a series of bloody encounters between Russia and Chechnya. Russian troops sought entry to Chechnya through Dagestan during the conflict. Russia's use of long-range weaponry for attacks on land and by air meant that many Chechen cities and villages were destroyed. Chechen civilians were especially vulnerable. In Dagestan, Chechen insurgents took hostages at a hospital in the city of Kizlyar. Throughout the conflict, thousands of refugees fleeing Chechnya sought shelter in Dagestan. Finally, a cease-fire between Russia and the Chechen rebels was signed in the Dagestani city of Khasavyurt in 1996.

In the devastation that accompanied and followed the war, Chechnya became a fertile ground for anti-Russian movements and extremism. This coincided with the rise of a militant form of Islam called Wahhabism, which found traction in Chechnya. Islamist rebels called for a holy war to ignite all of the northern Caucasus, much like the Murids had done in the 1830s.

In August 1999, Chechen separatists invaded Dagestan with the intention of creating an Islamic republic. This insurgence was a major factor in Russia's decision to launch the Second Chechen War. For 10 years, hostilities and guerrilla fighting beset the region. Bombings and attacks targeted the Russian military stationed in Dagestan. Moscow eventually declared its operation in Chechnya complete in 2009. However, a formal peace agreement was never reached. Both Chechen wars resulted in widespread deaths and casualties, especially among civilians. It is estimated that as many as 100,000 died in the conflict. Its reverberations continue to affect the northern Caucasus region.

In the years since the Chechen Wars, Dagestan has been the setting of frequent bombings, kidnappings, assassinations, hostage situations, and other violent attacks carried out by separatists, crime gangs, and Islamist extremists. Many of these attacks are aimed at Russian military, administrators, local

When Chechen militants entered Dagestan in 1999, they were met with resistance from local communities. Later, Russian artillery, seen here, poured into Dagestan to quash the invasion.

police, and religious leaders. Infrastructure, such as railways and natural gas pipelines, have also been targeted. Dagestan's interior minister, Adilgerei Magomedtagirov, was assassinated in 2009 at a wedding in Makhachkala. In 2011, a BBC News article called Dagestan "the most dangerous place in Europe." However, the heightened period of violence came to an end soon after. Since then, improvements in the economy and political changes have brought a greater sense of stability to the region.

Dagestan did again made international headlines in 2020 as the COVID-19 pandemic swept across the world and illness and deaths spiked in Dagestan. Many blame a delayed response from the republic's authorities as the cause of the virus's devastating impact on Dagestan. In the early days of the pandemic, Dagestanis continued public meetings, worship, and large celebrations such as weddings and funerals with few restrictions. In addition, official statistics failed to match up with the actual number of sick and dying in Dagestan. This gave residents a false perception of the risks of public gatherings. When the extent of the crisis became apparent in villages, local councils, called *jamaats* (jah-mah-AHTS), organized resources and provided guidelines for their communities that significantly curbed the spread of the virus.

INTERNET LINKS

https://www.smithsonianmag.com/smart-news/chechnya-dagestan-and-the-north-caucasus-a-very-brief-history-26714937/
Smithsonian Magazine presents a brief overview of the long history of tension between Russia and those seeking independence in the North Caucasus.

http://whc.unesco.org/en/list/1070
This web page details the ancient city of Derbent's impressive history, archaeology, and status as a UNESCO World Heritage Site.

https://www.youtube.com/watch?v=U6KR4cLLVzQ
Watch as author John Green explains the Russian Revolution and Russian Civil War in an episode of "Crash Course: European History."

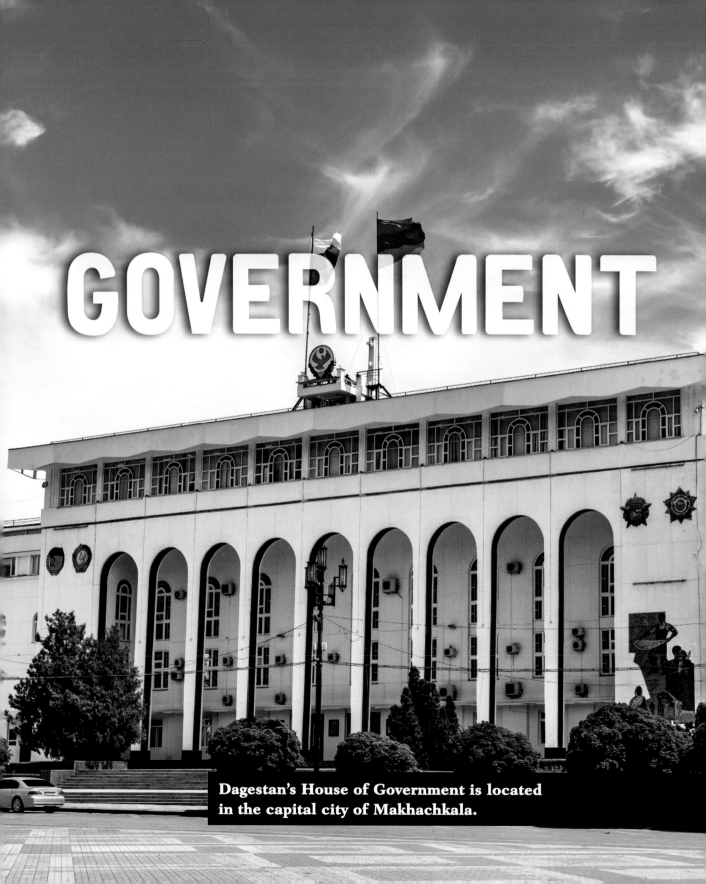

GOVERNMENT

Dagestan's House of Government is located in the capital city of Makhachkala.

3

THE PEOPLE OF DAGESTAN HAVE been woven into the fabric of Russian life, identity, and government since Dagestan was annexed by the Russian Empire in the 19th century. Dagestan's status has shifted from province to republic, with varying degrees of independence and autonomy. From 1921 to 1991, it functioned within the framework of the Union of Soviet Socialist Republics (USSR), or Soviet Union. Just before the USSR collapsed, Dagestan's parliament declared independence as a sovereign state and became the Dagestan Soviet Socialist Republic. On December 17, 1991, it was renamed the Republic of Dagestan.

The following year, on March 31, Dagestan joined other newly independent former Soviet republics in signing the treaty that created the Russian Federation. With this historic act, Dagestan again became part of Russia. Politics and government in the region since then have been shaped by the challenges of operating as both a republic and a part of the larger Russian Federation.

● ● ● ● ● ● ● ● ● ● ● ● ●

"We, the multinational people of the Republic of Dagestan, are a constituent part of the multinational people of the Russian Federation, historically united into a single state, conscious of our responsibility for preserving the unity of Dagestan."

—From the Constitution of the Republic of Dagestan, 2003

Dagestan is one
of 22 republics
within the Russian
Federation. The
republics are
regions that
were originally
composed of
non-Russian
ethnic groups.

RELATIONSHIP WITH RUSSIA

Dagestan's borders have shifted slightly several times since the czarist period. Despite the changes in its official boundaries and official name, Dagestan was and still is a part of Russia. Even though there are 14 languages recognized by the state, Dagestan's main language is Russian.

To be more specific, Dagestan is one of the Russian Federation's "constituent units," or subjects. Since 2014, Russia has claimed to have 85 constituent units with equal ties to the federation. Each of these subjects has its own leader, its own constitution or charter, and an independent lawmaking body. Subjects are grouped into eight large federal districts. Dagestan is in the North Caucasian Federal District, along with the Republic of Chechnya, the Republic of Ingushetia, the Republic of Kabardino-Balkaria, the Republic of North Ossetia, the Republic of Karachayevo-Cherkessia, and Stavropol Krai.

That means that Dagestan is under the control of the federal authorities, as are all members of the federation. The federal districts were created in 2000 partially to give officials in Moscow more control over the constituent units. The system of federal districts also helped establish order and a central authority for a sprawling realm that had partially lapsed into chaos after the USSR broke up. As a constituent subject of the Russian Federation, Dagestan sends its own representatives to the Federal Assembly's two chambers, the State Duma (the lower house) and the Federation Council (the upper house).

At the helm of each federal district is a presidential representative who is appointed—without the approval of the Federal Assembly—by the president of Russia. The individuals who fill these roles are called plenipotentiaries. Plenipotentiaries have great political and economic influence in the district and great authority over how regional governments are run.

Many of Russia's constituent units, including Dagestan, are still building their economies. They rely on the federal government for money and assistance. In 2017, Dagestan was the most subsidized republic in Russia. That year, about $896 million came to Dagestan from the Russian federal budget. Most of the remaining portion came from taxes within Dagestan and the republic's sale of land and small enterprises. As with many states, that money is not enough to sustain the republic through the year. In past years, as much as 70 percent of Dagestan's budget has been federally subsidized.

BRANCHES OF GOVERNMENT

As in the other republics that are members of the federation, Dagestan's system of government mirrors the structure of the federal system. A separation of powers is established in Dagestan's constitution. It defines the roles of the legislative, executive, and judicial branches of the government.

Dagestan's legislative branch contains the People's Assembly. This is composed of one house, or chamber. Currently, 90 representatives from Dagestan's districts are elected to a 5-year term in the People's Assembly.

The executive branch is made up of the Government of the Republic of Dagestan and its Head. The Head, also known as the president, is the highest official in the republic and serves a 5-year term. Individuals are recommended for this position by the president of the Russian Federation and approved by the

Members of the People's Assembly gathered in March 2019 to hear the annual address of the Head of Dagestan.

People's Assembly. The Government of the Republic of Dagestan is the main administrative body in the republic and is organized into ministries.

Dagestan's judicial branch consists of the Constitutional Court, federal courts of general jurisdiction (of which the Supreme Court is at the helm), and arbitration courts, which deal with business matters. The Superior Arbitration Court is the top-ranking body in the arbitration-courts system. All judges are appointed for life by authorities in Moscow, a practice many resent but that others view as politically prudent given the regional and ethnic interests that often divide the republic.

Vladimir Vasilyev was confirmed by the People's Assembly as Head of the Government of the Republic of Dagestan in 2018. He is not originally from Dagestan but was born in Moscow.

THE PROBLEM OF REPRESENTATION

More than 30 ethnic groups reside in the Republic of Dagestan. Due to this complex and diverse range of peoples, the political structure in Dagestan has faced unique challenges. To maintain fairness, order, and a sense of equality among the groups, the government institutions were originally formed to reflect the percentage of the population each ethnic faction represents. This plan was adopted to avoid rivalries and conflict among ethnic groups.

It has not always worked smoothly, and the republic's 1994 constitution was amended, or changed, several times before being replaced in 2003. In turn, that constitution has also been amended in order to establish the current government structure. The system is still far from perfect, and ethnic rivalries continue to threaten Dagestan's stability.

Originally, the executive branch of the government was the 14-member State Council with representatives from each of Dagestan's most populous ethnic groups. The State Council was responsible for electing a chairman from its ranks. This was intended to be a collective presidency in which leadership would rotate through the 14 major ethnic groups.

In the end, many in Dagestan felt that a balance of power among the various ethnic groups could not be achieved with the existing structure of

In 1998, the People's Assembly voted to change the part of the constitution that forbade the election of a State Council chairperson from the same ethnic group for two continuous terms. The new amendment merely limited the number of terms an individual chairperson could serve. This opened up the possibility of one ethnic group holding power indefinitely. Magomedali Magomedov, chairman of the State Council at that time, pushed for the change. In 1996, he had initiated another amendment that added two years to his first term in office.

Magomedali Magomedov was chairman of the State Council of Dagestan until 2006. Magomedov is seen here to the right of Russian president Vladimir Putin.

These changes provoked strong reactions among the people. Protestors rallied, claiming that the amendment made it possible for any given ethnic group to amass a disproportionate amount of power. Such a possibility would be dangerous to Dagestan's unity and weaken the foundations formed during centuries of struggle, growth, and compromise. In response to these concerns, both the State Council and the position of chairman were abolished in 2006.

the State Council. As a result, the People's Assembly voted to remove both the State Council and its chairperson from Dagestan's executive branch in 2006. Instead, the Head of the Government of the Republic of Dagestan became the main authority of the executive branch.

The wide-ranging ethnic makeup of the people of Dagestan has also had a great effect on the legislative branch. From 1999 until 2007, seats in the People's Assembly were divided up so that the 14 most populous ethnic groups were represented according to the relative size of their populations. That changed in 2007 to embrace a party principle instead. Today, deputies are elected from various political parties in an effort to more fairly represent all people in the republic. Those parties include United Russia, Fair Russia, and the Communist Party of the Russian Federation. However, achieving balanced and equal representation in government remains a challenge in Dagestan.

LEVELS OF GOVERNMENT

Administratively, Dagestan is divided into 51 municipalities, with 41 districts and 10 cities. Among Dagestan's cities, the largest is the capital city, Makhachkala. It had a population of 722,300 people in 2017. Makhachkala is one of the biggest ports on the Caspian Sea, connecting Central Asia with southern Ukraine and the rest of mainland Europe via ferries, railroads, and highways. It is also Dagestan's administrative center. Other prominent cities under the republic's jurisdiction are Khasavyurt, Derbent, and Kizlyar.

Citizens of Dagestan are constituents of concentric rings of government, beginning with local government. Local governments take account of the

Voters in Kizilyurt, Dagestan, went to the polls in the midst of the COVID-19 pandemic in July 2020. Members of the federation voted on changes to the Russian constitution.

structural and decision-making traditions of Dagestan's indigenous peoples. They have the power to resolve local issues. From small to large, the levels of government in Dagestan include the local government, the government of the Republic of Dagestan, the North Caucasus Federal District, and the Russian Federation. These levels reflect the multi-layered reality of Dagestani identity. It is shaped by ties to an ethnic group or village, to Dagestani nationality, and to Russian citizenship.

INTERNET LINKS

http://www.constitution.ru/en/10003000-02.htm
You can read the full text of the Constitution of the Russian Federation on this website.

http://nsrd.ru/
Visit the official website of the People's Assembly of Dagestan, the republic's parliament.

http://president.e-dag.ru/konstitutsiya-rd
Read an English translation of the text of Dagestan's constitution, accepted by the republic in 2003.

https://www.prlib.ru/en/node/420926
The online archives of the Boris Yeltsin Presidential Library offer a view of the constitution document adopted by Dagestan in 1994.

ECONOMY

About 275,000 people in Dagestan are employed in agriculture. That accounts for 30 percent of the republic's workforce. Many of them raise sheep and cattle.

4

D AGESTAN HAS CONSISTENTLY BEEN among the poorest republics in the Russian Federation. The wealth of the average Dagestani is only about a quarter of the average Russian wealth. Political instability and the wars and conflicts that have gripped the region have made economic prosperity elusive. Dagestan is a territory rich in natural resources, artisan goods, and raw potential. However, determining the best way to access and capitalize on these resources in a way that benefits the people of Dagestan has been challenging.

The republic's Soviet past has added to the difficulties in strengthening its industrial and economic base. At one time, Dagestan's economy existed to support and bolster the Soviet Union. During the years of Soviet domination, all commercial enterprises in the various republics were closely interconnected.

With the fall of the Soviet Union, these close ties were broken, and it became immediately evident how weak Dagestan's economy was. Businesses collapsed without the Soviet support on which many industries

From May to September in 2017, around 360,000 tourists flocked to the shores of the Caspian Sea in Dagestan. It is estimated that tourist accommodations along the coast are 95 to 100 percent full in the summer months.

had grown to depend. Many goods needed by consumers and business owners alike became unavailable or in short supply.

Until the period from 1996 to 1997, Dagestan's economy showed little sign of recovery from the sudden collapse of the Soviet Union. Then, as the Russian economy started to improve, Dagestan's followed suit. However, the upturn did not last long.

In the summer of 1998, Russia experienced another financial crisis. The Russian currency, the ruble, was devalued. Although that ruined some businesses—export firms in particular—and claimed many people's savings, it also helped small- and medium-sized enterprises in agriculture and the food-processing industry to develop.

Dagestan possesses a multi-industry economy. Agriculture, food processing, manufacturing, energy, and raw materials extraction are the main spheres of the economy. Of those, the agro-industrial sector makes the largest contributions to Dagestan's gross regional product (GRP)—the value of all goods and services produced in the republic.

A GROWING INDUSTRY

Agriculture accounts for about 20 percent of Dagestan's GRP. Roughly 55 percent of Dagestan's population lives in rural areas, and the majority of those citizens make their living through agriculture. Workers and officials are trying to make farming ventures more productive and efficient. Animal husbandry makes up the majority of all agricultural activities in Dagestan. Sheep breeding remains the main focus, especially for mountain residents for whom herding has been the main source of income for generations. Still, cattle breeding has gained in importance, and there are a few pig farms.

Planting and harvesting have always been challenging for Dagestan's agricultural workers. Due to poor, often infertile land, native residents often had to trade or barter goods to obtain grain. In the past, they bargained with Russian and other merchants, as well as with the Cossacks living in the lowlands of northern Dagestan. These types of exchanges still go on today. They have become standard for the Dagestanis living in the mountains and in the lowlands.

The irrigated lowlands are fertile and produce a variety of crops, including winter wheat, corn, sunflowers, potatoes, melons, and grapes. Still, only about 12 percent of Dagestan's land is arable. Because of this, priority is given to growing vegetables and fruit, especially grapes. Orchards of peach, apricot, plum, cherry, and other fruit trees are grown. The fruit is sold not only in local markets but throughout Russia as well. These ventures contribute considerably to the Dagestani economy.

Wine making is one of the traditional occupations of Dagestanis. It was and still is an important branch of the economy. Dagestanis even make a type of brandy that was highly prized in the days of the Soviet Union. The brandy comes from a Derbent distillery. Recently, Dagestan and the Russian federal government committed to greater efforts in developing this aspect of the republic's economy. Now, it is one of the largest segments of the food production industry in Dagestan.

There are more sheep than people living in Dagestan.

Dagestan is also graced with numerous bodies of water and aquatic life. In the Caspian Sea and in the river deltas and lakes, there are valuable reserves of fish, including sturgeon, salmon, herring, and trout. Fish processing used to be one of the most important industries in Dagestan, but overfishing has substantially reduced the size of the catches and posed a challenge for those who make their livelihood at sea.

IMPORTANT RESOURCES

Industry in Dagestan is quite diverse and includes aspects of oil and gas ventures, chemical manufacturing, construction, the production of machinery and tools, glassmaking, transportation, communications, textile manufacturing, fishing, food processing, and wine making. Part of the machine-building industrial sphere is also bolstered by the Russian military defense industry.

Sturgeon, a prized commodity in the fish market, are bred at a fish factory in the village of Yurlovke. Strict measures protect the endangered wild sturgeon in the Caspian Sea from overfishing.

The main industrial facilities are concentrated in the republic's largest cities, mostly in the capital of Makhachkala, which is also one of the biggest ports on the Caspian Sea. Derbent and a few of the other major urban centers—Buynaksk, Kizlyar, Kaspiysk, Khasavyurt, Izberbash, and Kizilyurt—support their own significant manufacturing and industrial base. These important economic centers, with the exception of Buynaksk, are connected by the main railroad and highway. Food-processing enterprises are scattered throughout Dagestan and are commonly found near large farms, vineyards, and ports.

The economy has shifted its focus significantly in the 21st century. The manufacturing of machinery and the food-processing industry have been reduced, while the energy sector's contribution to Dagestan's industrial output has risen. Dagestan, like the entire region surrounding the Caspian Sea, has

> # THE ALCOHOLIC BEVERAGE INDUSTRY
>
> *Dagestan is the second greatest producer of grapes in the Russian Federation. Dagestan's abundant grape yields have led to the success of wineries. As a result, the alcoholic beverages industry is a steadily growing area of food production. Wine, brandy, and cognac make up the bulk of alcoholic beverages produced in the region. Brandy and cognac are liquors made from distilled wine. Notable companies boosting Dagestan's economy with their success are the Kizlyar Brandy Factory, the Makhachkala Winery, the Derbent Brandy Factory, and the Derbent Plant of Sparkling Wines. Derbent is the central hub of alcohol production in Dagestan.*

some oil and gas deposits. Their existence has been known since ancient times when natural leaks brought the resources to the surface. Dagestan estimates that its natural reserves contain 509.3 million tons (462 million metric tons) of oil. In 1924, exploratory drilling initiated by the Soviets began in earnest. They started to extract oil on a commercial basis in 1936. Up to the end of the 1950s, the main sites were in southern Dagestan, but starting in 1958, the center of the industry moved to the Nogay Steppe in northern Dagestan. The vast infrastructure of Dagestan's oil industry—including its oil-extraction facilities, pipelines, and power plants—was built during the Soviet period.

Today, the oil and natural gas industries are concentrated near Makhachkala and Izberbash. The oil, besides being used and refined in Dagestan, is transported to other regions of Russia as well as abroad. Currently, natural gas is available as an energy source in 80 percent of Dagestan, and the republic plans to continue expanding its natural gas infrastructure.

Dagestan has abundant natural reserves of building materials, including limestone, marl, gravel, sand, and clay.

HYDROELECTRIC POWER

Dagestan's hydroelectric power stations have the potential to produce a lot of electricity. Several hydroelectric power plants have been built along the Sulak River. Many in the region have already been in operation since the middle of the 20th century. The most powerful of these is the Chirkeyskaya hydroelectric power plant.

The Chirkeysk Reservoir lies on the other side of the Chirkeyskaya Hydroelectric Dam, which began producing electricity in the 1970s.

Large plants are also found on the Kara Koysu at Gergebil as well as along the Terek River at Kagarlinskaya. Besides the Chirkey Dam, the Sulak River also has hydroelectric power plants at Chiryurt and Kizilyurt. Dagestan's power plants are able to satisfy the region's energy needs. The republic is also connected via power lines to the rest of Russia and is able to export some energy to other parts of the federation.

BUILDING CONNECTIONS

Geographically, Dagestan is well situated, connecting Russia with the rest of Asia via the Caspian Sea. For centuries, an important trade route wound through the region. The city of Derbent was built along this route to protect the merchants who used it.

Today, the republic's transportation infrastructure is much more extensive. Dagestan is connected to the rest of Russia, as well as to Azerbaijan and Georgia, by railroads, airports, and highways. Some roads and railways were built in the late 1800s. A main railroad line stretches from Baku to Astrakhan via Derbent and Makhachkala. The route then splits, with one branch heading north along the Volga River and the other winding its way to Kazakhstan. A different branch goes from Makhachkala to Gudermes, near the Chechen capital of Grozny, through Stavropol and then via Rostov-on-Don to Moscow and to Kharkov in the Ukraine. Altogether, there are about 342 miles (550 km) of railway in the republic. So, despite its rugged and often inhospitable terrain, Dagestan is well connected to the world beyond its borders.

Paved roads total more than 4,970 miles (8,000 km). Unpaved roads are more common in the mountain regions where the small population, lack of industrial centers, and difficult terrain make it hard to create a major or highly developed system of highways, which would also be costly to maintain. Important highways that cross through Dagestan include the Rostov-Baku highway, the Astrakhan-Makhachkala highway, and the Caucasus highway. The Moscow to Baku thoroughfare was built long ago and is of international importance. Other important roads are located along the Caspian shoreline as well as between Makhachkala, Grozny, and Stavropol.

A significant port on the Caspian Sea, Makhachkala draws merchant and fishing fleets and is the site of a major terminal for transporting oil from sea to land. The port underwent reconstruction starting in 2005. It links with the rail system through the use of ferries. Makhachkala also has an international airport just outside the city. The capital's developed infrastructure has made Dagestan a major transportation and communications hub in the North Caucasus and Caspian Sea region.

ARTISAN CRAFTS

Traditional handicrafts are a significant, though small, part of Dagestan's economy. Since ancient times, the people of Dagestan have been known for their handicrafts. Many villages specialized in a certain trade and became known for it. Some communities were famous for their sheepskins or for their tools made of steel, iron, or copper. Others were well known for their rugs. Some villages developed expertise in fashioning jewelry or sabers and other weapons, while some enclaves produced pottery.

The industrialization of the economy resulted in widescale handicrafts and folk practices dying out. Still, many traditional crafts persist in Dagestan, as the region's ethnic groups contribute their artistic styles and types of handicrafts. The handicrafts of Dagestan are a rich legacy that forge a connection to the past and offer a means of honoring and extending the traditions to future generations. While in the past many handicrafts resulted in the creation of something practical and useful in the family's everyday life, today many of these objects have taken on the status of art. For example, the Lezgin and Tabasaran peoples make rugs that are highly prized, while the villages of Kubachi and Gotsatl are famous for their distinctive, glittering pieces of jewelry.

NEW DIRECTIONS

Poverty has been a persistent problem in Dagestan. In the fall of 2004, 1.366 million Dagestanis—65 percent of the population—had an income below the poverty line. Alleviating poverty has become an overriding concern since then. Social and economic government programs have focused on developing businesses of all sizes; bolstering transportation systems, like oil and gas pipelines; and adopting legislation to promote and encourage increased investment. However, old clan rivalries and general corruption have frequently stood in the way of progress. Black-market operations and some businesses' failure to report revenue have impeded economic growth and stability.

A newer sphere for economic advancement includes various improvements in communication. Dagestan is committed to bridging the digital divide that currently exists in many parts of the republic. Plans are underway to make high-speed internet readily available across the republic. This can be achieved through the construction of fiber optic communication lines and the installation of WiFi shared access points.

Tourism is an exciting field in Dagestan with promising possibilities for economic growth. Makhachkala is a popular destination for visitors, easily accessible by plane and train. From there, travelers can take in the stunning mountain landscapes of southern Dagestan, explore ancient and cultural sights, or find healthful relaxation at the seaside or one of Dagestan's many mineral springs. Dagestan has also become a popular attraction for those interested in extreme sports tourism. Numerous opportunities for mountaineering, hiking, rock climbing, ice climbing, and rafting draw adventurous travelers to the republic's many wild regions. Accommodations for travelers can be found in Dagestan's growing number of hotels, spas, and guest houses.

Participants in the 2020 Yarydag Festival, named for Mount Yarydag, traveled to Dagestan to soak in its natural beauty and test their mountaineering skills.

INTERNET LINKS

https://eng.russia.travel/dagestan/
This national tourism website provides a guide to all the best spots for tourists interested in Dagestan, whether they're seeking cultural, extreme, beach, or food adventures.

https://www.themoscowtimes.com/2018/08/24/dagestan-hosts-sheep-beauty-queen-contest-a62657
For a republic whose economic fate is tied so closely with that of its livestock, sheep have a lot of significance. This 2018 article in the *Moscow Times* chronicles a "Sheep Beauty Queen Contest" that took place in Dagestan.

ENVIRONMENT

Maintaining the natural beauty and balance of Dagestan's environment is an ongoing challenge.

5

THE RICH AND DIVERSE NATURAL features of Dagestan are among its greatest assets. However, the toll of industrial activities and global climate change are becoming more apparent in Dagestan. As the tourism industry grows, Dagestan has an added economic incentive to preserve and protect its natural environment. The natural heritage of the region is even more important for those indigenous groups who have been stewards of the land for millennia.

Poor drainage systems, especially in Dagestan's highland villages, can increase contamination and pollution.

Rapid industrialization in Dagestan and the northern Caucasus during the 20th century led to the pollution of many valuable resources, most notably the Caspian Sea. More efficient and well-planned scientific approaches to agriculture and water management are needed as Dagestanis work to protect the environment for the future.

CONTAMINATION IN THE CASPIAN

Pollutants have been discharged directly into the Caspian Sea. They also pass through municipal water collection and treatment systems that are unable to filter out many contaminants. Through the years, toxins have reached levels that are dangerous not only to the many

aquatic species living in the sea but also to the people living along or near its shores. Dagestan's water collection and treatment systems are in need of investment capital for improvements. In addition, the creation of new environmentally sensitive factories and facilities would benefit the environment.

Overfishing in the Caspian Sea has also overtaxed the ecosystem. Strict regulations, especially in regard to endangered sturgeon, have been implemented to restore balance to the sea. However, these restrictions have posed significant challenges for fishermen who depend on local catches for their livelihood.

The Caspian Sea provides vital resources for fishermen in Derbent. The government keeps track of fish species to ensure sustainable practices.

POLLUTED LANDS

The republic's valuable land and soil resources have not escaped the harmful influence of industry either. Chemical plants, oil-extraction facilities, and coastal fish-processing operations account for a large portion of the environmental damage. The many hydroelectric power plants built along the rivers have damaged biological resources in the interior as well, although to a lesser extent. Reducing industrial pollution is a top priority in Dagestan's attempts to improve the environment.

There are other urgent problems as well. In some areas, particularly in the Nogay Steppe, where water reserves are low, erosion and desertification have radically transformed the face of the land. The salinization, or increased salt content, of the soil is another grave development. The land bears the stress of a fast-growing human and livestock population as well as the increased cultivation of more and more acreage. Short-term solutions initially eased the impact and damage but ultimately only added to the salt levels in the soil. In a vicious cycle, this process has led to even more extensive desertification in some areas.

Sturgeon roe is sold as caviar. Despite fishing regulations, sturgeon is peddled on the black market.

Wars, most recently between Russia and Chechen militants, have also been a major cause of environmental degradation in Dagestan. The use of military weapons has scarred and poisoned the land. The cost of cleaning up afterward has been immense.

INVESTING IN THE ENVIRONMENT

Dagestan has invested in renewable energy as a way to curb damage to the environment and build a more sustainable future. In addition to hydroelectric power plants, solar power offers renewable energy opportunities. With about 310 days of sunshine a year, Dagestan's climate may provide an excellent field for solar power. A solar power plant was built in Kaspiysk in 2013 with the capacity to produce a large amount of energy. The potential for expanding

Industrialization has negatively impacted Dagestan's environment. Shown here is air pollution near the city of Derbent from a tire factory in the 1990s.

MELTING GLACIERS

The long-term impacts of global climate change in Dagestan have recently become apparent. One area of concern is the effect of rising global temperatures on mountain glaciers. Dagestan's major rivers flow from the mountains of the Greater Caucasus range to the Caspian Sea. They are fed by glacial melt that occurs every year. A cycle of glacial melt in the spring has meant that rivers have seasonal floods. This pattern facilitates the irrigation of agricultural fields. However, rivers are in increasing danger as average temperatures continue to rise and break down mountain glaciers. Changes to flooding and dry periods will result. If glaciers continue to melt and retreat year-round, the effects on the environment of Dagestan will be dramatic.

Lakes, rivers, and glaciers in the Caucasus Mountains must be protected from the effects of global climate change.

geothermal energy resources in Dagestan also offers a new direction in energy production.

A commitment to safeguarding the environment has also taken form in the expansion and creation of nature reserves. The Dagestansky State Natural Reserve (also known as the Dagestan Nature Reserve) is the largest in Dagestan. It covers several different territories and preserves the natural habitat of hundreds of native species. In addition, Dagestan has 3 federal nature sanctuaries, 12 regional nature sanctuaries, 3 state nature parks, and 27 regional natural landmarks that are protected by the government.

INTERNET LINKS

https://phys.org/news/2019-04-caviar-oil-caspian-sea-pollution.html
The unique biosystem of the Caspian Sea extends beyond its Dagestani coastline. This article explores the pressing challenges of pollution and climate change.

https://wwf.ru/en/regions/the-caucasus/the-caucasus-hotspot-sustainable-forest-management/
The World Wildlife Fund is committed to protecting the forests of the North Caucasus. This web page outlines threats and recommendations for the region.

https://wwf.ru/upload/iblock/e71/dagestan_eng.pdf
This 2016 survey of the state of glaciers in Dagestan provides a closer look at the environmental challenges facing the republic.

"Glaciers will eventually retreat both in the west and east of the region, with changing natural conditions no longer able to sustain them; the snow line will climb increasingly higher into the mountains. These small glaciers can be expected to disappear by the end of the 21st century."
—A. A. Aleinikov and O. N. Lipka, *Dagestan: Melting Mountains*

DAGESTANIS

People from Dagestan often wear traditional
clothing for performances and special events.

6

Chamalals are the smallest ethnic group in Russia. They live in Chechnya and Dagestan.

DAGESTAN HAS ONE OF RUSSIA'S fastest growing populations. More than 3 million people now live in the republic. They have a mix of backgrounds, religious traditions, and values. Many are indigenous peoples whose ancestors have lived on the land for centuries. Others belong to outside nationalities and ethnic groups who have settled in the area in recent generations.

The mountains that dominate southern Dagestan are home to a wide variety of tribes who have thrived in the region. Many have since moved to the flatlands, but they work to retain their cultural traditions, customs, and community ties. Some of these tribal groupings are small, consisting of between 1,000 and 2,000 members. Adding to this diversity are the peoples and ethnic groups that have lived mainly in the lowlands and the cities. Most Dagestanis are Muslim, but small portions of the population are made up of Russians, Ukrainians, and other primarily Christian nationalities. A small Jewish population is also present.

HERITAGE AND ETHNICITY

The republic's largest ethnic group is the Avars. They represent about 29 percent of the entire population of Dagestan. They live mainly in the mountainous and hilly regions of western and central Dagestan. They

The Mountain Jews have Iranian, or Persian, origins in their ancestry and language. They are sometimes classified as Tats.

are followed by Dargins, who make up about 17 percent of the populace, Kumyks (about 15 percent), Lezgins (about 11 percent), Laks (about 5 percent), Tabasarans (about 4 percent), Azeris (about 4 percent), and Russians (about 3 percent).

All of the peoples living in Dagestan are culturally similar, since most of them have interacted with one another for centuries. An overwhelming majority also practice the same religion—Islam. They are all Dagestanis, but they can be divided into three large groups that correspond with the languages they speak. These ethno-linguistic groups are classified as Dagestanian, Turkic, or Slavic. The three groups give an indication of the common roots many ethnic tribes share.

Caucasian people speak Dagestanian languages, which are a branch of the North Caucasian family of languages. This family of languages is spoken by other people living in the Caucasus region, mostly in the northern districts of Azerbaijan, in some villages of Georgia, and in the republics of Chechnya and Ingushetiya. The Dagestanian languages themselves are subdivided into several related languages. For example, the Avars speak one form of Dagestanian languages, Lezgins speak another, and the Laks and Dargins share a separate form. These forms are further divided into dialects.

Turkic language groups are also represented in Dagestan. The Nogay peoples are Turkic groups that came to the northern Caucasus in the 13th century. They now live near Dagestan in the Stavropol, Chechnya, and Karachayevo-Cherkessia regions. Kumyks also speak a Turkic language. They have historically occupied northern parts of Dagestan, especially the Kumyk plateau and areas near the South Terek River and Caspian Sea. Azeri, or Azerbaijani, people speak a Turkic language and traditionally live on both sides of the Dagestan and Azerbaijan border.

The Slavs speak Slavic tongues, mostly Russian and Ukrainian. In fact, most Dagestanis are bilingual. They use Russian in their everyday lives in addition to ethnic languages. Residents of remote mountain villages are a notable exception. They have little exposure to or use for Russian in their day-to-day existence. Most people who live in the mountain villages today are indigenous to these areas. Their families have lived there for thousands of years.

DAGESTAN'S MOUNTAIN JEWS

Mountain Jews traditionally lived in the mountain villages of Dagestan or the larger cities of Makhachkala, Derbent, Buynaksk, and Khasavyurt. It is believed that they came to the North Caucasus from Israel. Evidence of their life in Dagestan—such as cemeteries with Jewish gravestones—dates back to ancient settlements. Their culture has combined Persian and Jewish traditions with those of the North Caucasus.

People belonging to this particular ethnic and religious group were the subject of deliberate discrimination in czarist and Soviet Russia. Some fled Russia to escape persecution while others stayed in Dagestan. Many of those who remained were classified as Tats during the secularization of the Soviet period.

Mountain Jews are a dwindling group in modern Dagestan. Violent attacks aimed at Jewish communities and leaders have urged many to emigrate. Estimates indicate that only a few hundred Mountain Jews are still living in Dagestan, mainly in Derbent and Makhachkala.

Dagestan has a unique situation in that many small minority groups make up the bulk of its population. This unusual breakdown has helped to ensure the strength and survival of distinct ethnic identities. At times, conflicts have divided the region and pitted groups against each other. However, Dagestani tribes have largely been able to live peaceably side by side for centuries. In addition, Dagestanis have embraced a broader Russian identity while still maintaining and nurturing their ethnic roots.

"We did not come to Russia voluntarily and we will not leave voluntarily."

—Rasul Gamzatov, Dagestani poet

INTERNET LINKS

https://minorityrights.org/
Use the search box to look up the ethnic groups of Dagestan on the Minority Rights Group International website.

https://www.ruptly.tv/en/videos/20190226-011-Russia-Drone-captures-ancient-Avar-mountain-village-in-Dagestan
View drone footage of the architecture and layout of Koroda, an abandoned Avar village built between the third and fourth century CE.

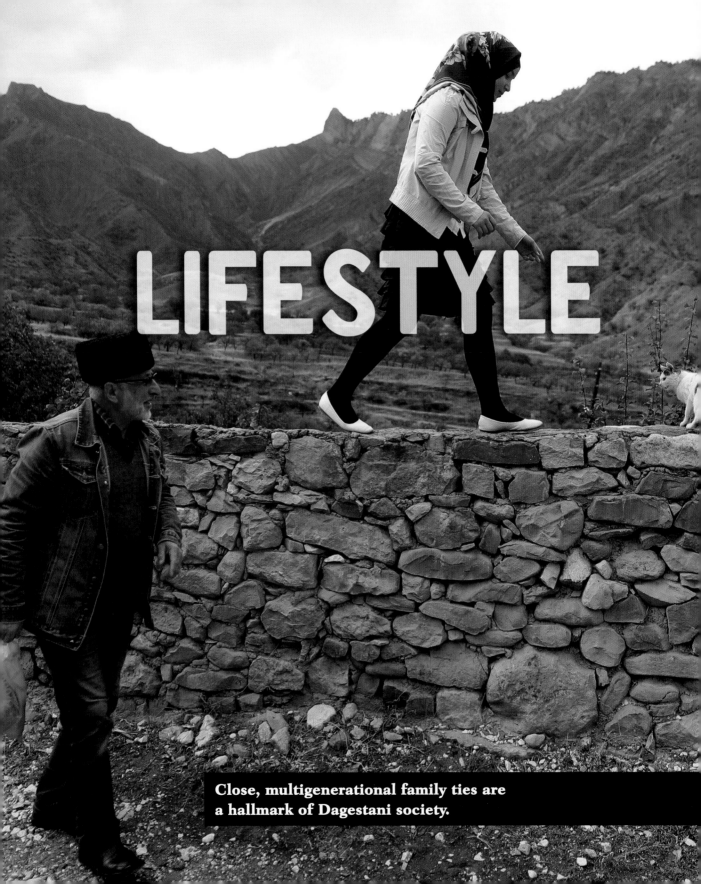

LIFESTYLE

Close, multigenerational family ties are
a hallmark of Dagestani society.

7

I N THE MOUNTAIN VILLAGES OF Dagestan, life is steeped in tradition. Old customs and beliefs influence many of the activities and interactions that make up daily life. For most Dagestanis, Islamic practices exist side by side with the ethnic customs and values of their home village. Living in close proximity to other ethnic groups has also contributed to the merging of customs between Dagestan's indigenous peoples.

The mountainous terrain and historic resistance to invasions in Dagestan have shaped the lifestyles and character of the people. Social and political changes have influenced their lifestyles as well. During most of the 20th century, all non-Russian cultures were affected by Soviet dominance. This had both positive and negative consequences.

Modern Dagestan is a complex mix of the old and the new. People's lifestyles often depend on income. The gap between city and village life is striking, as it is in many other parts of the Russian Federation. Most women work outside the home while at the same time shouldering the main responsibility for household chores. This adherence to tradition can lead to challenges for women in Dagestan.

Traditions are honored and respected, particularly in rural areas, where most of the populace lives. As a result, ancestral mores and ways have powerfully influenced Dagestani culture as a whole. To this day,

Namus (nah-MOOS) means "support" or "the ability to give." It lies at the heart of the unwritten moral code of the Dagestani people. A person with *namus* is generous, reliable, affable, compassionate, and conscientious. *Namus* forms the cornerstone of family and community life in Dagestan.

respect for the older generations and the past is a keystone of the culture. Despite the republic's long and turbulent history, many of the customs and traditions of Dagestan have survived for hundreds and thousands of years. While cultures and lifestyles have grown increasingly similar throughout the Russian Federation, many of Dagestan's indigenous peoples have worked hard to maintain their own unique traditions and cultural identity.

FAMILY

The typical Dagestani family is a nuclear grouping, consisting of a married couple and their offspring. Rural dwellers tend to have larger families than people living in the city. In cities and villages alike, though, boys traditionally enjoy a higher status than girls. Dagestani society is highly patriarchal—lineage is traced through the father's side. Traditionally, the father and husband is head of the family. He is responsible for the well-being of family members and also for managing all their property and assets. Although both men and women typically work, it is the men who must ensure financial security for the family. Thus, they typically have the final say in decisions within the family. Only rarely does a woman become the head of a family. This does happen in special circumstances, such as when the male head of the household dies or moves abroad in search of work. In such cases, the oldest woman then assumes responsibility for the family's well-being.

More often than not, particularly in rural areas, young people live with their parents until they marry. After marriage, young men try to settle as close as possible to their parents' home.

Grandparents maintain close contact with their children and grandchildren, helping the new families with household chores and with the upbringing of children. Occasionally, elderly parents move in with their children, typically with their son's family, thus enabling the young to take better care of the old. Small children, as soon as they are able, are expected to help their grandparents.

Polygamy, or the practice of multiple marriages, has a long history in Dagestan. Traditionally, both Islam and Judaism permitted polygamy. Among Jews, rabbis and wealthy men typically had two wives when the first wife was unable to bear children. Muslim men could have up to four wives. Although forbidden by law, polygamy among Muslims still exists in Dagestan, mainly in rural areas. Women in polygamous relationships often have little influence on their husband's decisions. Fearing abandonment, they may submit to their spouse's behavior and guidance in order to maintain the union.

CLANS

Several families from the paternal side form a *tuhum*, or clan. The size of a tuhum depends on the ethnic group. Some are made up of as few as 5 families; others consist of as many as 70. In keeping with Dagestani society's patriarchal nature, a tuhum is rarely headed by a woman. Instead, it is typically headed by an authoritative man, selected on the basis of his personal qualities and experience and the role he plays in the life of the community. In some ethnic groups, the oldest male is chosen as the head of the tuhum.

Within the clan, the care and protection of relatives are among the most sacred duties. Clan obligations include the extended family as well, and members are expected to take care of nieces and nephews, cousins, and even great-aunts and great-uncles. The role of the tuhum is particularly significant during major events in a person's life. At such times, members of a tuhum support one another financially, contributing when someone builds a house, celebrates a wedding, or organizes a funeral.

The clan assumes responsibility for the behavior and actions of all of its members. The clan takes pride in every member's achievements just as the whole clan is also culpable for every member's misdeeds. The practice promotes unity as the clan shares its members' glories and disappointments. If a serious problem arises, the head of the family summons a family council, in which the elders have the final word.

COMMUNITY BONDS

In the past, poverty and hardship have made it difficult to survive without the support of close community bonds. As a result, people have developed ties not only within their extended family but also with their neighbors and the other residents of their village or town.

During the COVID-19 pandemic in 2020, local *jamaats* and charities helped organize the distribution of food and necessary supplies to those in quarantine.

Any individual or family in a Muslim village can receive assistance from their *jamaat,* or local rural community. When someone's house is destroyed by fire or a mudslide, for instance, the community provides all possible support, including the financial means to get the victims on sure footing once again. People also help one another by picking crops, shearing sheep, and building houses. Family, friends, and neighbors only need to be asked to help, and they do what is within their means. People are expected to help one another willingly and with pleasure. Even the elderly, who may be unable to contribute physically, encourage and cheer on the workers. After work, everyone enjoys a large festive meal, prepared by the host family.

Dagestani villages still have councils of elders, which consist of the most highly respected members of the community. In the past, these councils, relying on customary and Islamic laws, regulated a wide range of social issues. During the Soviet era, however, the role of these councils in Dagestani village life became significantly weakened.

In cities, community ties are somewhat weaker than in rural areas. However, mutual bonds are still strong in comparison to those in many Western nations or in regions that make up the rest of the Russian Federation. City dwellers in Dagestan keep in close touch with their families, friends, and neighbors, providing one another with the support necessary to successfully navigate their daily lives.

WELCOMING GUESTS

As one popular Dagestani expression states, "Even if a guest comes unexpectedly, he is never unexpected, because we are waiting for a guest always, every day, every hour, and every minute." With such a sentiment, it comes as no surprise that hospitality and the ability to be a welcoming and gracious host are highly prized values in Dagestani society. The best bed, the best food, and the best seats at the table are all reserved for guests. Moreover, if a guest expresses his or her fondness for an object in the house, he or she is typically given it as a present.

In the Caucasus, a special term exists to describe a guest—*kounak* (koo-NAHK). A traveler of any origin and religious background, no matter whether he or she comes from a friendly community or a rival faction, a kounak is always received with the highest honor and dignity. He or she is unquestionably offered an overnight stay, food, and personal safety; and the visitor's belongings are always ensured protection. A kounak maintains close contacts with their host family, and if he or she stays repeatedly at the same house, he or she becomes an honorary kounak. Such a person then has the opportunity to become even closer than a family member. An honorary kounak is invited to the most important family events and participates in making important decisions. Choosing to stay overnight with other people subsequently becomes an insult to the host family. The title of honorary kounak is also hereditary, or passed down from parent to child.

HOMELAND

To say "I swear by this soil" is the most sacred oath a Dagestani can make. The homeland is considered a sacred place. Even if people raised in rural settings move to faraway cities, they try to preserve the house built by their ancestors, often high in the mountains, and pass it on from generation to generation. Children are brought to see the land of their ancestors and to listen to the stories told about their grandparents by village elders. Before dying, many Dagestanis express a wish to be buried in their home village.

Away from their homeland, Dagestanis attempt to stay in touch with compatriots. Moving to a new place, they form communities where they attempt to preserve the atmosphere of their homeland. As a rule, relations among Dagestanis living abroad tend to be strong. Dagestani expatriates speak the language of their ancestors and preserve Dagestani traditions and customs. In different parts of the world, people of Dagestani origin have been known to change their names to Dagestanly to honor their heritage. Even far away, this abiding unity makes the Dagestani feel accountable to their family and to their entire clan. This feeling of responsibility is often a great incentive to work hard and to achieve prominent positions in society.

CHILDHOOD

Dagestan has one of the highest birth rates in Russia, and it is rare to see a Dagestani family without children. The birth of the first child is cause for celebration. If it is a boy, a huge feast is held, and guests come to offer their wishes of health and happiness for the newborn and his mother. The birth of a girl, in contrast, is usually celebrated only in the family circle.

Naming a child is a serious matter. Names are believed to influence fate and thus are chosen carefully. Many Dagestanis believe that a name gives spirit, determines the child's future life, and provides lifelong protection. Both health and luck depend on a person's name. Therefore, Dagestanis often name their children after legendary national heroes or deceased family members who enjoyed a long life. Recently, parents have started to give their children the names of their grandparents or highly respected family members who are still alive. The name is announced to a circle of friends and family members who gather in the newborn's house. An esteemed guest takes the baby in his or her hands and pronounces the child's name three times. If the baby is a boy, "Grow up, *dzhigit* [brave one]! Be like the person whose name you carry!" is proclaimed. In particular, the residents of the village of Kubachi have a strong belief in the power of names. If a child was thought to be delicate, parents have been known to change their name in the hope of imbuing the child with a stronger constitution.

All the milestones in a child's life, including the first tooth, first haircut, and first step, are celebrated. When the baby turns 40 days old, the family cuts the child's hair and nails. The appearance of the first tooth is also cause for blessings and praise. In some parts of Dagestan, a baby's first step is the time when a father tests his child's willpower. If the baby makes the first steps in front of the father, the father gives them a gentle nudge, and the child falls to the floor. If the child is able to get up without help, a feast follows. If the child fails to get up, they are sent to the house of friends or relatives. After several days, the child is brought back home, and the ritual is repeated until the child is able to stand up on their own.

Girls and boys are brought up differently, and an extensive network of people take part in their respective upbringings. A girl usually spends a lot of time with her mother and the other women in the family. She is brought up to be patient and taught that she will be dependent on her husband. From early childhood, a girl performs household chores. In southern Dagestan, where the art of carpet making is especially popular, girls also learn how to make these elegant textiles.

These children in Dagestan are wearing traditional school uniforms. About 600,000 children in Dagestan attend school.

In contrast to girls, boys are brought up to be the future head of their family. While boys also help their parents, their workload is limited, which leaves them plenty of time for games and sports. Boys start working later in life. Sons of craftsmen start learning the secrets of their father's profession from age 12. Diligence is the main virtue parents hope to pass on to their children, both boys and girls.

SCHOOL

Dagestan possesses an increasingly educated and skilled modern workforce. During the Soviet period, Dagestan—like all other regions in the former Soviet Union—achieved near total literacy. Education was modeled after the Soviet system and, at higher levels, was conducted mostly in Russian. This was an immense achievement for a place where, just a few decades earlier, most of the tribes did not even have their own written language. Although some groups used Arabic script to write in their language, the practice was not widespread.

In primary schools, some children were taught in their local language, though students were required to learn in Russian. Since Russian was the

To attend a university in the Russian Federation, students must pass a Unified State Exam (USE) in Russian.

official state language of the USSR, it also became the predominant language of instruction in high schools and universities. That status has changed little today, as Russian continues to be the language of education, politics, and everyday life.

In the early 1890s, there were eight primary schools in all of Dagestan (which had a population of less than a million people at the time) with a little more than 200 students enrolled. In addition, there were religious schools in village mosques where pupils learned Islamic law under the guidance of a mullah. Religious schools, however, were suppressed during the Soviet era. By the end of the 1980s and just before the collapse of the USSR, Dagestan had more than 1,500 primary, middle, high, and vocational schools. Enrollment totaled more than half a million pupils. In addition, the republic had four institutions of higher education, including Dagestan State University and Pedagogical Institute, now called Pedagogical University. A branch of the USSR Academy of Science, with its four research institutes, was established in Dagestan. Any Dagestani could go to any Soviet educational institution in the country, but they had to compete to gain admittance to a particular institution. Education, even at the university level, was free.

A lot has changed since then. Educational reforms have been attempted. However, schools have increasingly charged tuition, and corruption dogs the system as it does many other institutions in Dagestan. Today, the education system is in need of improvement. Some initiatives have been introduced, but slowly and with much resistance from various groups who feel the changes will negatively impact their access to learning.

A rise in Islamic education has been facilitated by Middle Eastern Islamists. They poured money into Dagestan in the 1990s in order to build madrassas (schools for Islamic instruction) and mosques. Religious education is reestablishing itself in the republic.

MARRIAGE

Dagestanis have always treated marriage with seriousness and ceremony. Traditionally, young people did not leave their parents' home before they were married. A young man chose his future wife from several candidates suggested by his parents. Following his selection, his family named certain high-powered intermediaries to negotiate with the girl's parents. In most ethnic groups, people married inside their clan, and very often, they married their cousins. This was shaped mostly by financial considerations: Clans did not want to lose the property they had held for generations. Occasionally, members of different clans intermarried. In general, though, negotiators discussed the size and the form of *kalym*, the gifts that the groom had to supply the bride's parents to ensure that the girl's needs were met and to cover related expenses. Successful negotiations were followed by an engagement and marriage.

These traditions have gradually begun to change. More and more often, young people find partners of their own choosing, and marrying within one's own ethnic group or clan has become less of a social or economic imperative. Although some people still prefer to subscribe to this once traditional pattern, inter-ethnic marriages are common in the republic's cities. While Dagestani women usually marry men from other Dagestani ethnic groups, Dagestani men more and more often marry Russian, Ukrainian, and Belarusian women.

Cohabitation is uncommon. A couple can opt for a civil nonreligious marriage ceremony, but most choose to have a religious one as well. Unwritten laws guide the financial arrangements of the marriage. To share the costs of the ceremony, parents appoint trustees among close friends and family. As a rule, only happily married couples are asked to help organize a wedding, as this is believed to bring good luck to the young couple. Trustees partially share the expenses. The groom's parents are traditionally responsible for providing the young family with housing, and the family of the bride is responsible for furnishing the interior of the newlyweds' home. Today, young couples often decide where to live on their own.

The attitude toward separation is also changing. Divorce has gained wider acceptance and become more common. Divorce rates are higher in urban areas because cities have relatively more liberal social norms and a higher ratio of Slavic peoples for whom the practice has lost much of its stigma. Nevertheless, Dagestan still has one of the lowest divorce rates in Russia.

WEDDING CELEBRATIONS

A Dagestani wedding is a big feast, to which all family members and friends are invited. While city dwellers send bright invitation cards to their friends in the mail, a specially selected person goes from house to house to spread the word in villages.

Weddings are typically celebrated in early fall, between the traditional times when grapes were harvested and then turned into wine. The unions are celebrated when the weather is warm enough for people to stay outside and when fruit and vegetables are in abundance. Food is cooked in large amounts, so that no one leaves the feast hungry. Alcohol consumption is limited, as public drunkenness is frowned upon.

At an Islamic religious ceremony, the imam reads a special prayer and tells the young couple, "In joy, in separation or in sorrow, always remember the blessedness of marriage and the first embrace. Forget about the last quarrel." A Christian religious ceremony, held in a church, often has a solemn touch. In front of the altar, the couple swears to be faithful to each other and to love each other until death.

Marriage celebrations usually start simultaneously in the houses of both the bride and the groom. The bride's departure from her parents' house and her arrival at the groom's house are a major part of the festivities. First, the groom's delegation arrives at the bride's house to the accompaniment of songs. Parting with her daughter, the mother gives her advice and wishes her happiness in marriage. Soon, the wedding procession, with family and friends in tow, leaves for the groom's house. If his house is not far away, the festive crowd walks. Carrying torches, family and guests play music and compete in games. Jesters perform funny sketches. The women from the groom's family carry presents and sing, praising the young couple, as well as the bride's father and brothers.

In cities, the wedding procession consists of beautifully decorated cars, and drivers repeatedly honk their horns to attract everyone's attention. The future mother-in-law meets the bride with the following words: "May you bring us happiness and wealth; may you not die before you see your great-grandchildren at your knees." To demonstrate their happiness, the groom's family meets the bride with an ancient dance. People throw nuts, grain, candy, and coins at the bride.

"Dear bride and groom," the *tamada* (tah-mah-DAH), the master of the wedding ceremony, says, "it is a very important day. Many guests have gathered here in this room. Now you should thank your parents, the organizers of the wedding. Give them a bow for everything they have done to bring you up. Give them a bow for their blessing!" Guests, especially the couple's parents, often meet these words with tears. The couple then gives their parents a deep bow to express their love, respect, and sense of duty. The celebration extends late into the evening.

Weddings in Dagestan are colorful and often elegant affairs. Feasting and dancing are main ingredients of the festive day.

Preparing the bed for the couple's first night, women roll a small boy on the newlyweds' bed and ask God to bless the young couple with sons. The next morning, women bring the bride new clothes and take away her old dress. The bride then prepares breakfast for her new husband and his friends, and the feast goes on for three days.

TRADITIONAL ROLES FOR MEN AND WOMEN

Yag' (YAKH), or masculinity, is a concept that stands at the core of the traditional ethical code of Dagestani men. This notion comprises honor, dignity, courage, fortitude, diligence, honesty, nobility, generosity, respect for the elderly, and kindness to the weak and the poor. Yag' also implies patience, tidiness, and duty. According to this code, a man is not expected to complain about thirst and hunger, cold and heat. He is not allowed to show signs of tiredness when talking to an elder. A man is discouraged from showing his fear. In addition, a man's superior status is unquestioned and does not need to be proved. His role as the head of the family supports his dominant position. Most traditional Dagestani women respect a man's authority.

A Dagestani boy is brought up according to these principles. Starting in his teen years, he learns the ethical code through socializing in the

godekan (ghoh-deh-KAHN), the village square. There, he also learns to develop humility and self-control—qualities highly valued in a land of extreme ethnic diversity and economic hardship.

Traditionally, a Dagestani woman is taught from an early age to be a hostess, a mother, and a guardian of the home. A Dagestani woman is often subjected to the more traditional demands of being modest, obedient, and patient. She is expected to serve and honor her husband and please her mother-in-law. A young woman must also agree with the decisions made by other family members and abide by family rules.

Despite these tightly defined expectations, women have always occupied a place of honor in Dagestani society. Men watch their language when they are next to a woman, no matter how old she is. Furthermore, women gain authority and status with the passing of time and the attainment of old age. Elderly women participate in decision making as much as men do. When an elderly woman enters the room, men get up from their seats to show their respect.

During the Soviet era, women received more rights than ever before. Many Dagestani women pursued advanced degrees, started working outside the home, and occupied positions at the middle and higher administrative levels. Although there are women employed in government posts today, they are heavily underrepresented. In the fields of education and medicine, women represent the majority. Nevertheless, even those working outside the home are typically responsible for taking care of their children, for cooking, and for performing household chores. Thus, most Dagestani women bear a heavy workload.

Economic hardships make it necessary for some Dagestani men to move to other parts of Russia. While some do only seasonal work away from home, others leave their families for longer periods of time. The migration of male workers also takes place within the republic. Those living in rural or mountain communities, unable to find work close to their homes, move to the plains or

According to traditional Dagestani values, a woman should aspire to devotedness, diligence, modesty, loyalty, and good upbringing.

HORSES IN DAGESTAN

The horse has been central to Dagestan's rural and mountain dwellers for centuries. Even today, some remote mountain villages can be accessed only on horseback. Traditionally, a guest, upon arriving, first offered praise to the host's horse. In the past, some ethnic groups killed a horse after the death of its owner. The meat could be served as part of the funeral feast. Wild horses can still be seen roaming the high plateaus and hillsides of Dagestan. Horse racing and horse-riding tricks are also celebrated activities. They are often a lively component of festivals and special occasions.

to urban areas. As a result, more and more often, a woman becomes the head of the family and primary breadwinner.

ELDERS

Dagestani children learn to respect not only their parents but also all elders. They are taught to view the older members of their communities as a source of wisdom and experience. Thus, older people hold a special place in Dagestani society. They are the first to be served food and the first to speak. Their advice is usually heeded by those seeking counsel and direction.

In public transportation, young people typically give up their seats to elderly passengers. People also avoid smoking in the presence of the elderly. Disrespect for the elderly is frowned upon and is heavily criticized. The phrase "Let your old age be not needed by anyone!" is among the gravest insults. "Let God give you a long life for us!" is what an elder would prefer to hear instead.

Dagestan is known for having many centenarians, people who are at least 100 years old. Most centenarians live in the intermediary mountain ranges, which are those at an altitude of 5,250 to 6,560 feet (1,600 to 2,000 m) above sea level, but centenarians can be found across the republic. The elders are revered by the whole community and extended family, which consists of their children, grandchildren, and great-grandchildren. These century-old individuals are often praised for their good memory and bountiful sense of humor. Many

Dagestan's Magomed Labazanov was believed to be the world's oldest man when he died in 2012 at age 122.

A historic cemetery in Derbent is filled with carved Muslim tombstones.

demonstrate an exuberant zest for living and are often eager to give advice to the young.

DEATH

Elders who feel that death is impending often organize their own memorial and prepare their own grave. Following Islamic tradition, the deceased is buried in a white piece of cloth before sunset on the day of the death. Someone who dies in the afternoon is buried the next day. If the death occurs in a room, the room is smoked to purify it, and all of its contents are brought outside into the sunlight. Distant relatives tend to visitors who come to express their condolences. In some ethnic groups, women visit in the morning, while men visit in the afternoon.

A funeral procession follows the body to the cemetery. Also according to Islamic practice, women follow the coffin only a short distance because they are not allowed to be present at the burial. Women offer up songs of mourning, often accompanied by tears. Men are not supposed to cry in public. The family of the deceased orders a *zikriad* (zee-kree-AHD), or funeral prayer, which is intoned in Arabic on the grave. After the funeral, the prayer is read in the house of the deceased. Then, a memorial meal is served separately for the men and the women.

Villagers cancel all celebrations until the family of the deceased gives its consent for them to resume. If a young person dies, villagers will not celebrate weddings until an acceptable amount of time has passed. The immediate family of the deceased wears for some time the clothes they had on at the moment of their relative's death. Women usually dress in black, and men do not shave. Elderly women wear a dark-colored headpiece, and elderly men wear a *papakha* (pah-PAH-khah), a traditional tall astrakhan hat. Memorial days are observed on the 3rd, 7th, and 40th days after death, and then one year after death.

Slavs bury their dead in coffins, usually on the following day or within two days after the death. Those who come to express their condolences or attend the funeral are offered candy. Christians invite a priest or a religious figure to read a prayer over the deceased. Memorial observances are marked on the 9th and 40th days after the death.

Differences in Christian, Jewish, and Muslim burials can be seen in the tombstone design. Muslim tombstones are generally notable for their tall and thin shape. The language of the inscription on a headstone can give clues to the religion of the deceased as well. Gravestones in Dagestan are often seen with elaborate, detailed carvings.

INTERNET LINKS

http://www.olyaivanova.com/editorial.html?line=dagestan
View a gallery of photographer Olya Ivanova's images from daily life in the villages of Dagestan.

https://www.rbth.com/arts/travel/2013/10/10/attending_a_traditional_dagestani_wedding_uninvited_30067
This article provides detailed descriptions and images of traditional wedding activities in Balhar, Dagestan.

https://ru.boell.org/en/2020/04/15/oni-tozhe-mechtali-istorii-dagestanskikh-zhenschin
From 1994 until 2009, a Dagestani doctor named Aishat Magomedova operated a free women's hospital in Makhachkala. This website tells her story and presents a 2019 documentary called *They Also Had Dreams* about women in Dagestan.

RELIGION

Muslims pray at a mosque in Makhachkala.
Most of the existing mosques in Dagestan were
built after the fall of the Soviet Union.

8

The Grand Mosque in Makhachkala has the capacity to hold 17,000 worshippers. It is one of the largest mosques in the Russian Federation.

MORE THAN 90 PERCENT OF Dagestan practices Islam. The culture and politics of Dagestan have been strongly influenced, especially in recent years, by the Islamic identity of most of its citizens. The overwhelming majority are Sunni Muslims. A small percentage, usually belonging to the Azeri or Tat ethnic groups, are Shiites. Some of the greatest challenges in modern Dagestan today are related to the rise of fundamentalist Islamic groups and the government's response to them.

Christianity is represented in Dagestan as well. Ethnic Russians, Ukrainians, and Belarusians are often Orthodox Christians. Small groups of Baptists and Protestants can be found in the north, while Armenian Gregorians (followers of the Armenian Apostolic Church) and Catholics are mainly found in the larger cities. Judaism is practiced by a small portion of the population as well. At times, the religious practices of Jews, Muslims, and Christians in Dagestan have blended with older, pagan-based rituals specific to the region.

SPIRITUAL DEVELOPMENT

Different religions have contributed to the spiritual development of the Dagestani people. In the fourth and fifth centuries, Orthodox Christianity came to Dagestan from Byzantium, Armenia, Georgia, and Caucasian Albania. Nevertheless, the local population remained largely unconverted. In parts of Dagestan where some groups eventually came to accept Christianity, the new religion was combined with old pagan rites, though eventually this hybrid belief system disappeared.

Judaism became firmly established in Dagestan in the fifth and sixth centuries with the arrival of the Tat-speaking Jews from Iran. The faith was supported by the Khazar Khanate. Although Judaism became a state religion in the Khazar region in the eighth century and took root in northern Dagestan, it never became widespread. The fall of the Khazar Khanate around 965 reduced the influence and practice of the religion in the future republic. Today, this

The Armenian Church of the Holy Savior in Derbent was built in the 19th century. Few churches survive from earlier periods.

religion is practiced by Mountain Jews and Dagestan's Ashkenazi Jews, who emigrated from Russia in the 1800s.

Islam took approximately a thousand years to establish itself in the region. The Arab expansion in the seventh century brought Islam to Derbent. From there, it spread to the southern and southeastern parts of Dagestan. In western Dagestan, Islam became prominent in the 15th to the 17th centuries. As Islam became increasingly important, the influence of native and pagan religions receded. Over time, many pagan beliefs merged with Islamic traditions. Islam became even more strongly rooted in Dagestan when foreign mullahs were gradually replaced by local ones.

Sufism and the Sufi order Nakshbandia also played a role in the region's gradual embrace of Islam. Sufism is a mystical branch of Islam that accentuates internal belief. It took hold in Dagestan beginning in the early 18th century. Sufism was used for political purposes by imams during the Caucasian War and began taking shape as a religious and political doctrine under Imam Shamil. *Gazavat*, armed defense and struggle against the unfaithful, was emphasized. This particular aspect of Sufism soon led to a religious zeal that swept the region.

Islam continued to flourish in Dagestan despite the victory of czarist Russia in the Caucasian War in the mid-19th century. In 1861, Dagestan had 1,628 registered mosques and 4,000 mullahs. By the beginning of the 20th century, there were more than 2,000 mosques. One of Dagestan's main printing houses of the time, in the town of Temir-Khan-Shura (present-day Buynaksk), published religious books in *ajam*. Based on Arabic script, *ajam* allowed for books to be published in local languages.

The Russian Revolution of 1917, however, brought this religious development to an end, and all religions were equally affected by the ensuing political changes. Churches, synagogues, and mosques were either closed or destroyed. Islamic religious schools ceased to exist, and thousands of mullahs were barred from practicing their faith if not executed. By 1985, there were only 27 officially functioning mosques, 5 churches, and 3 synagogues left in Dagestan. Nonetheless, dozens of underground religious institutions continued to function "illegally" throughout the Soviet era.

Muslims who flaunt
religious traditions
can lose their right
to be buried in the
village cemetery.

ANCIENT RITUALS

Despite the long Islamic tradition and the framework of the monotheistic, or single deity, religions that became established in the region, Dagestani culture carries many traces of its pagan roots. Some Dagestanis, when they turn to God for help, perform pagan rituals often accompanied by Islamic prayers.

Paganism has left its mark on agricultural practices as well. Some ethnic groups historically perform rituals to fight the drought and to increase the harvest. These practices are found especially in the more rural precincts. In such a rite, one of the villagers is undressed and covered with grass and green branches. A procession of young people attaches a rope to the chosen person and walks him through the village, joining in a special song about rain.

Instead of a person, some ethnic groups use a doll named Zemire, or Andir-shopai, an old name for the god of rain. If this rite is ineffective, villagers find the bones of a horse and bring them to a mullah. The mullah then reads two prayers: one asking God to send water from the sky and the other asking him to provide plenty of water in the wells. After the prayer, people take the bones to a well and wash them. The bones should not be immersed in water; otherwise it will never stop raining.

Pagan beliefs also designate certain areas and places as sacred. In southern Dagestan, a grave of a saint is called *pir* (PEER). In the north, it is called *zyarat* (zy-ah-RAHT). There are several hundred such graves, crowned with cube-shaped mausoleums. These graves can be seen from a distance, marked by long sticks with flags and pieces of colorful material attached to them. Those who are ill pray at the sacred sites for good health. Childless women may come to seek the blessing of pregnancy, while other believers seek out the sites in search of good luck.

RISE OF ISLAM

With such a large Muslim population, Dagestan is seen as a bastion of the faith. In the years since the Soviet Union collapsed, the republic has witnessed the widescale restoration or construction of mosques and Islamic schools throughout its territory. The revival of Islam is especially strong in the central and northern parts of Dagestan. On Fridays, men above the age of 14 gather in mosques. Nearly all villagers, except for pregnant women, the sick, and small children, fast during the month of Ramadan. Individuals often take part in religious rites and keep up with their faith on account of social pressure.

In the south, however, the situation is different. Some villages have no restored mosques and no one to organize Friday prayers and sermons. Therefore, in some Lezgin, Lak, and Tabasaran villages, the function of mosques is replaced by sacred places, such as the sacred mountain Shalbuzdag.

The hajj (pilgrimage to Mecca in Saudi Arabia) and *umra* (small pilgrimage) have become increasingly popular since the 1990s. Minibuses, decorated with Arabic writings and Saudi souvenirs, regularly travel via Iran, Turkey, Syria, and Jordan to bring hajjis to Saudi Arabia. To avoid accidents, bus drivers make stops at sacred places to pray with the passengers for a safe trip.

A branch of Islam called Wahhabism has considerably destabilized Dagestan since its appearance in the region in the 1980s. Followers of

Officials in Dagestan have often engaged in severe anti-terrorism campaigns that target fundamentalist Muslims.

It is not difficult to imagine why Shalbuzdag is considered a sacred mountain. An atmosphere of mysticism pervades the area.

Muhammad ibn Abd al-Wahab, Wahhabites are Sunni radicals and extremists fighting to spread their particular vision and interpretation of Islam. The movement originated in Saudi Arabia and has been especially active in neighboring Chechnya. In Dagestan, there have been significant conflicts between Wahhabites and Sufis. In September 1999, the Dagestani parliament adopted a law banning the Wahhabites and other extremist organizations from the republic. Salafi is the more common name today for the branch of fundamentalist Islam that includes Wahhabites. Still, only a small percentage of Dagestanis embrace radical Islam and its calls for violence.

The Islamic revival took a new turn in Dagestan with the rise of two new radical elements: the Caucasus Emirate in the North Caucasus and the Islamic State in the Middle East. Estimates indicate that up to 5,000 Dagestani Muslims have been recruited by the Islamic State. They have left Dagestan to live and fight mainly in Syria and Iraq. The call from radical Middle Eastern Muslims for solidarity has especially appealed to young Muslims in Dagestan. Some have gone to carry out violence in what they see as a holy war. Others seem to have

The Juma Mosque in Derbent is the oldest mosque in Dagestan. It was built in the year 734 in the place where an old Christian basilica once stood.

MUSLIM CUSTOMS

Travelers to Dagestan should be mindful of local Muslim customs. Although requiring head coverings for Muslim women is not a universal and historical feature of Dagestani culture, the practice has recently been widely adopted. Women travelers, especially those visiting the villages, are encouraged to wear long skirts and head scarves as a gesture of respect. Women should not smoke in public places or shake hands with local men as a greeting. It is more typical for men and women to greet by nodding at each other. Modest clothing for men, especially pants instead of shorts, is also recommended. Both women and men are encouraged to only drink alcohol conservatively and avoid public displays of affection between couples. In large cities like Makhachkala, these guidelines are more relaxed, but they can be followed as a sign of respect for local religious traditions and culture.

been attracted to the idea of living under statewide Islamic law. Dagestani citizens who joined the Islamic State are viewed as terrorists by the Russian government. Many have died abroad, but some have been disillusioned with the Islamic State and sought a return to Dagestan. They risk family separation and harsh prison sentences from the Russian government if they come back.

INTERNET LINKS

https://www.rbth.com/arts/327141-russias-oldest-mosque
Read about the history of the Juma Mosque, the oldest mosque in Russia and one of the few to survive the Soviet era.

https://rlp.hds.harvard.edu/religions
Navigate the Religious Literacy Project website to learn more about the beliefs of Islam, Judaism, and Christianity. These are the three main religions in Dagestan.

http://www.kaukaz.net/cgi-bin/blosxom.cgi/english/dagestan/maali
Read a traveler's perspective on the festive opening of a new mosque in the village of Maali, Dagestan.

Дербент благодари
президент
Российской Федераци
В.В. Путин
за набережну

LANGUAGE

A Russian-language billboard in Derbent thanks
Russian President Vladimir Putin for the
construction of a new embankment in the city

9

ALONG WITH HAVING THE GREATEST ethnic diversity in the Russian Federation, Dagestan is also the most multilingual republic. As many as 50 different languages are spoken there. There are 14 major languages connected with Dagestan's largest ethnic groups and dozens of dialects derived from them. Avar, Dargin, Lezgin, Kumyk, Lak, Azeri, Russian, Tabasaran, Chechen, and Nogay are the most prevalent ethnic languages. Although many of these languages are related, they are not necessarily mutually intelligible. Dagestani languages can be very complicated. Most are characterized by a great number of consonants, very few vowels, and complicated sound systems. Others have as many as eight genders, which affect verb conjugations and nouns.

Traditionally, Kumyk was the inter-ethnic language of trade spoken in Makhachkala. It was later replaced with Russian.

Historically, the tribes in Dagestan were arranged in villages that ascended the mountains and foothills. They practiced vertical polylingualism, which meant that they spoke the language of their own village and the language or dialect of the village below them.

Today, most Dagestanis are multilingual. They speak the language of their ethnic group, the local language of inter-ethnic communication (such as Avar, Kumyk, or Azeri), the Russian language, and sometimes the language of their neighbors (Chechen or Georgian). Russian is the undisputed lingua franca, the common language used by a wide variety of groups most often for government affairs and to transact business. Replacing the Roman alphabet with the Cyrillic alphabet in 1938 made Russian more accessible. By 1989, 61 percent of Dagestanis spoke Russian.

After Russian, Avar is the second most common language of inter-ethnic communication and the native language of 99 percent of Avars. The Avar language belongs to the North Caucasian language family. The number of dialects is so great that practically every village has its own. The literary (written) language is based on the so-called "language of the guest," which developed through the centuries via conversations with guests and in markets where residents of different villages interacted. Before Arabic ajam, the Avars used the Georgian and the Albanian writing systems. Five Dagestani languages—Avar, Dargin, Lak, Lezgin, and Tabasaran—have literary status, while others exist only in spoken form.

The evolution of Dagestan's languages is unique. For more than 4,000 years, many of the republic's dialects and languages have been spoken in the same locations where they are still in use today. One explanation as to why so many distinct Caucasian dialects and languages have been preserved is that their native speakers lived in scattered groups that had little contact with one another. Even the residents of some neighboring mountain villages—separated by deep and impassable gorges—often speak different languages. Some indigenous languages are spoken by no more than a few hundred people and are in danger of dying out.

WRITING SYSTEMS

The frequent changes to the writing systems used in Dagestan reflect its rich and turbulent linguistic history. At different times, cuneiform, the Caucasian Albanian alphabet, Gunn writing, Khazar writing, Arabic ajam, the Roman alphabet, and the Cyrillic alphabet have been used.

Caucasian Albanian, one of the two indigenous Caucasian alphabets, went out of use early in the region's history. Although scholars knew about the existence of this alphabet starting at the end of the 19th century, it only became an object of study half a century later, after the discovery of copies of the Caucasian Albanian alphabet used in Armenian manuscripts from the 15th and 16th century. Short writing on a stone slab in Azerbaijan was discovered as well.

Due to Dagestan's long tradition of Islamic culture and literature, many Dagestani languages were written in Arabic script. The oldest example of this kind is a group of notes in the Dargin language, written on the margins and between the lines of an Arabic manuscript from 1243 CE. Other examples of writing in Arabic script, as well as in Dargin, Lak, and Avar, date back to the 15th century. The Arabic alphabet ajam was used in Dagestan until 1928, when it was replaced by the Roman alphabet. In 1938, the Roman alphabet was replaced by the Cyrillic alphabet. Although Dagestanis usually learned to read and write in their own languages, most also mastered Russian as a second language. The Cyrillic alphabet that is still used includes the letter I, which existed in the pre-revolutionary Russian alphabet. Since this was the only letter that was added, some consonants in Dagestani languages are rendered through the combination of several Russian letters.

MASS MEDIA

Dagestan's mass media also reflects the republic's multilingualism. More than 400 print and electronic media outlets and sources are available and produced in Dagestan's various languages. That number includes 200 newspapers and magazines. While some print media sources are published in one language, others are translated into many. State television and radio stations broadcast in a variety of languages.

The majority of print media is controlled to some extent by the state. Administrative bodies on all levels use newspapers for disseminating information and conveying political purposes and intent. About 100 state and commercial television and radio channels are registered in the republic. Television has existed in Dagestan since the 1960s. A wide range of Islamic media outlets exists in Dagestan too. Some channels interrupt broadcasting during prayer. Most religious mass media covers social and political issues. Given the complex political situation in the Caucasus, the Muslim Spiritual Administration controls all religious mass media.

Many primary
schools teach in
ethnic languages,
but high school
and university
classes are all
taught in Russian
in Dagestan.

DAILY COMMUNICATION

Greetings and gestures play a crucial role in the day-to-day communications of Dagestanis. Over centuries, the social mores and conventions of different ethnic groups, typically sharing similar economic or religious backgrounds, have converged. Dagestani codes of behavior emphasize the demonstration of respect for elders and the difference between the social roles of men and women. In addition, special behavioral norms exist for communication on bridges and at malls, public ovens, bathing places, and streams.

A Dagestani always answers "Fine" when asked "How are you?" Social practice dictates that people should not complain, nor should they demonstrate that they are tired or bored, thirsty or hungry. When talking to someone, it is important for Dagestanis to stay friendly and calm. While working, people especially attempt to display a good attitude or mood. It is also deemed important for a person not to emphasize his or her personal input to a given task or project, and it is considered in poor taste to comment on another's work. In addition, employees look for ways to alleviate the workload or burden of others.

In rural areas, women and men, especially those who are not married, are expected to keep a respectful distance from one another. Therefore, communication between female and male villagers is often limited to a short greeting, sometimes followed by a question about the well-being of family members.

Gestures intensify the meaning of spoken words. Dagestanis often use them to express anger. Slapping one's hips and pinching express disdain, while pointing one's hands to the sky before covering the face with them expresses disappointment and contempt. Placing the hands on the hips and raising one's chest express superiority and independence.

Even communication on horseback has its own special rules. When meeting or crossing paths, riders are expected to show respect by rising halfway in the saddle. Meeting an older person, a rider slows down, rises in the saddle, and silently passes by, acknowledging that person with a glance. Meeting someone familiar, the rider dismounts the horse, takes off his hat, and greets them with a handshake and friendly words.

Conditions for ethnic languages to survive are best in the mountain villages where local traditions still govern social and cultural interactions. Throughout

As the largest ethnic group in Dagestan, Avars have banded together with initiatives to protect and celebrate their way of life. In 2011, they created the Avar National and Cultural Autonomy to promote Avar culture and language. Their initiatives include the distribution of print, internet, and television media in the Avar language. This group also helped launch Avar TV in 2013 to increase the broadcasting of Avar programs. Avar TV is based in Makhachkala, but it can reach a wide audience across Dagestan. Avar is both a spoken and literary language, meaning that it has a written form. In 2016, there were about 530,000 speakers of Avar. The language is made up of two dialect groups—northern and southern—with various subgroups in each.

Dagestan's history, the isolation of mountain villages has helped to preserve their native languages. Some dialects become threatened when villagers leave the mountains for urban and lowland areas. As mass media and improved transportation forge broader connections between traditional communities and the larger republic, it is necessary to preserve endangered languages.

INTERNET LINKS

https://www.britannica.com/topic/Caucasian-languages/Nakho-Dagestanian-languages
This article breaks down the categories of Caucasian languages spoken in Dagestan.

http://dagpravda.ru/
Visit the online publication of *Dagestanskaya Pravda*, a socio-political newspaper in the republic.

https://riadagestan.ru/
View news and headlines about the latest events in Dagestan on the website of the Republican Information Agency.

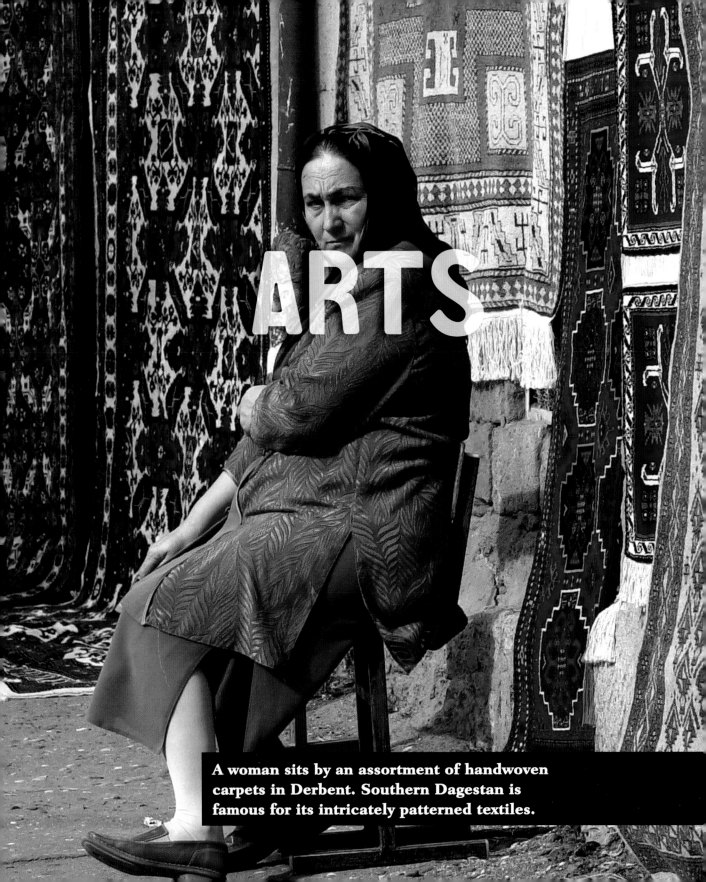

ARTS

A woman sits by an assortment of handwoven carpets in Derbent. Southern Dagestan is famous for its intricately patterned textiles.

10

A LARGE PART OF DAGESTAN'S RICH cultural tapestry is represented by the artistic talents of its people. In addition to accomplishments in literature, architecture, fine arts, and theater, Dagestan also excels in the decorative arts. Villages across the republic have gained a national reputation for the specialty goods they create. These include silverware, pottery, woodcarving, carpet weaving, and jewelry. Ropewalking, folk dances, and body tattooing are other creative expressions of Dagestan's artistry.

Many of these traditions have a long history. Excavations in different parts of the republic have shown that bronze was already widely used by jewelers 5,000 years ago. Fathers passed the secrets of their trade to their sons; mothers passed their skills to their daughters. Historians and travelers from around the world admire the beauty and craftsmanship of Dagestani handiwork, and for many years the work of Dagestani craftspeople has been exhibited in international museums.

"Feats of mountaineers, brotherhood and honor, There it was, here it is. My Dagestan and my Russia, Together with Thee forever!"

—From the State Anthem of the Republic of Dagestan

HANDWOVEN CARPETS

Dagestan is known around the world for its carpets. In response to the increased availability of mass-produced carpets that often replicate the traditional designs, women in the village of Tabasaran preserve the republic's long tradition of handwoven carpets.

The Dagestani art of carpet making dates back to ancient times. The oldest still-existing Dagestani carpet was made in the sixth century in Derbent. In the past, masters brought their carpets to the shores of the Caspian Sea. They believed that their work was complete only when the carpet had been washed by the sea waves and warmed in the sun. For centuries, light and thin carpets featuring different shapes, designs, and motifs—mostly in blue and red—have been an essential part of any Dagestani home.

METALSMITHS

Intricate designs are hand cut by Kubachi's metalsmiths to create jewelry and other decorative items.

In ancient times, the village of Kubachi was famed for making armor and chain mail. Three hundred years ago, it excelled in making daggers, swords, pistols, and guns. Today, Kubachi is renowned for its jewelry. No other place in the Caucasus can boast such excellent and delicate engraving techniques. Sometimes, black ornaments appear on a light silver background or vice versa.

The home of every master has a small museum or display highlighting examples of jewelry and pottery work from the past. While some of these works were made locally, others were brought from India and the Middle East. Exquisite scabbards and the hilts of old armaments, filigree jewelry, cigarette cases, wine vessels, caskets, goblets, vases, and trays all find their admirers in different parts of the world. The works of Kubachi masters have been exhibited in Saint Petersburg, Moscow, Brussels, Montreal, Osaka, and London. In 1937, Kubachi goldsmiths won the Grand Prix—a famous contest—in Paris.

POTTERY

The Lak village of Balkhar has specialized in ceramics since the 13th century. Originally emerging in the mountains as a simple means of earning a living, Balkhar ceramics turned into an art form. People from across the Caucasus bought the beautiful pottery made by the villagers.

Taught from an early age, Balkhar women were responsible for the entire pottery-making process, from finding the clay to firing a completed work in the oven or kiln. Men helped prepare the clay, repaired the ovens, and brought the finished pottery to the market and either sold it or exchanged it for other goods, usually from other parts of Dagestan or from Azerbaijan.

Balkhar residents make around 30 kinds of kitchenware, each with its own function: carrying water, heating milk, whipping butter, pickling cheese, or storing flour or grain. The kitchenware, diverse in its design, is distinguished by its rich ornamentation, thin walls, fine lines, and symmetrical forms. Potters coat their works with yellow and white clay. White clay tends to turn red after the heating process.

A yearly fair in Makhachkala allows young artisans to display their crafts and honor their cultural heritage.

Parisian
newspapers
called Tsovkra
ropewalking
"ballet on a rope."

Spirals, scrolls, and curves, as well as scenes of life in the mountains, embellish the distinctive pottery of the Balkhar residents. More recently, Balkhar masters have started making decorative plates and miniature statuettes as well.

WOOD CARVING

Although wood carving has been popular nearly everywhere in Dagestan, the village of Untsukul has won special fame in this area of expertise. For 200 years, Untsukul masters have been developing unique methods of decorating spoons, plates, and walking sticks. More recently, Untsukul craftspeople have started making frescoes adorned with plant and animal designs. These frescoes are typically used as home decoration.

ROPEWALKING

In the 1930s, daring ropewalkers brought fame to the tiny mountain village of Tsovkra when they turned a traditional practice into entertainment. Popular

Ropewalkers practice without safety nets both in studios and outside. A 20-foot (6 m) titanium pole is used for balance.

lore of Tsovkra claims that the day of a boy's birth is when he starts learning how to walk on a rope. According to legend, Tsovkra men stretched ropes over a precipice to shorten the way to goat and sheep pastures. With the passing of years, ropewalking became an art form.

A ropewalker, dancing a *lezginka* (lez-GHEEN-ka) on a thin cord, is an essential part of any Dagestani feast. As it was done centuries ago, brave men balance on a steel rope high above the ground, performing dangerous tricks without any safety measures, to the strains of *zurna* (zoor-NAH) and drums. The most spectacular trick is *farmingo* (fahr-MEEN-goh), in which four men stand on one another's shoulders and perform a back flip with their eyes covered. The athletes perform at weddings, holidays, and other special events.

In *lezginka*, men imitate the strong, proud movements of an eagle while women channel the grace and poise of a swan.

FOLK DANCES

The ability to dance is highly prized in Dagestan. In the past, when strict laws did not allow for free and open communication between the sexes before marriage, dances at weddings were an opportunity for young people to establish contact and to express their interests in and feelings for one

Lezginka productions by professional dance troupes are elaborately choreographed and costumed. The folk dance is also performed by ordinary people at weddings and other celebrations.

another. Certain gestures and glances carried special meanings. As dancing was believed to demonstrate one's dignity and dexterity, dancers were observed by potential in-laws.

The most famous dances are the saber dance and the lezginka. A saber dance features an explosion of nonstop energy. Men move around the stage, clinking their sparkling sabers with speed and precision.

Lezginka, arguably the most famous folk dance in the post-Soviet era, is an echo of older, pagan rituals in which eagles had a special meaning. The image and symbolism of the bird is portrayed by the male dancer when he balances on his toes, spreads his arms (to signify wings), and then circles them, as if preparing to soar. Dances performed by women are marked by grace and dignity. In contrast to the sharp, tempestuous movements of the men, the women look as if they are floating on air, moving gracefully and smoothly across the floor. In some dances, the woman cannot raise her hands higher than her waist. Only rarely can she throw a glance at her partner. The man looks at the woman as if he is trying to protect her. Throughout the dance, though, the overriding rule is that the man can never touch the woman.

CULTURAL TATTOOS

Body tattooing is one of the oldest traditions practiced by some ethnic groups living in the mountains of Dagestan. It serves several functions. Some tattoos were made to mark a woman as belonging to a certain clan or ethnic group. Other tattoos were used to show her age. Girls aged 13 to 15 were tattooed to indicate that they had entered the age of puberty. Tattoos are often placed on the face, hands, arms, legs, feet, or chest. Tattooing often had ritual and mystical meaning. For others, it is simply a form of decoration. Although each ethnic group and each village had its own tattooing patterns in the past, plants and animals were the most frequent motifs.

ARCHITECTURAL ACCOMPLISHMENTS

Most Dagestani cities and towns resemble stereotypical Russian urban centers, full of apartment blocks that can hardly be differentiated from one another. This style and model of urban planning was followed throughout the 20th century. However, the traditional architecture of Dagestan's mountain villages demands a closer look.

Mosques, watchtowers, signal towers, fortresses, and bridges dominate the Dagestani architectural landscape in the rural and mountainous communities. A number of arches and columns also characterize the architectural style. The wooden or stone facades of houses, mosques, and tombs are often carved. Despite the fact that Islam prohibits the images of people and animals from being portrayed, the carvings often depict beasts and birds, as well as hunting and fighting scenes. Special attention was traditionally given to the decoration of gates, often arch-shaped portals covered with traditional ornamentation. The entrances to some houses included inscriptions marking the date of the building's construction.

Dagestani architecture has been largely shaped by geography and the need of local residents to defend themselves from attacks. The key principles of

The Khan's Palace in the Naryn-Kala fortress of Derbent shows off pointed arches and architectural features that strenghthened its defense against invaders.

Dagestan's highland villages mirror the structure of the mountains around them.

house construction have stayed all but unchanged for centuries. Since early times, Dagestani villages, called aoul, have been founded high in the mountains and often look like an extension of their natural settings. Since there was little land that could be used for agriculture and grazing, people settled on the southern sides of gorges and rocks. Rectangular-shaped houses were built of stone, clay, brick, and wood.

Village construction did not follow any specific plan, so as to save space and to confuse attackers who would have trouble finding their way around the unfamiliar village. Normally, houses had one or two floors and a covered yard. Because of the lack of space, every square inch was utilized, and the flat roof of one house could serve as a neighbor's outdoor area or terrace. The ground floor of a house was usually reserved for typical household purposes.

The prince of the Subterranean Kingdom fell in love with a girl from Earth. The loving couple got married and decided to escape from the kingdom. The furious king ordered his subjects to catch the runaways. When the young couple saw the people pursuing them, they asked God to turn them into a mosque with a mullah. Their wish came true, and the king's people, having found nothing on Earth but a mosque with a mullah, returned to the Subterranean Kingdom.

The king realized that his son had fooled him and ordered that the pursuit be resumed. However, the pursuers returned to report that this time they had not seen anything on Earth but a couple of ducks on a lake. The king realized he had been fooled again. He issued the same proclamation, ordering the search party not to return without the runaways. When the young couple realized that they were still being pursued, they asked God to turn them into a boulder, and once again their wish came true. Since then, people have been honoring the boulder by coating it with fat.

The southern sides of houses often had built-in galleries, balconies, or loggias, which were sometimes protected with glass.

Looking at a village located on a faraway hill, the houses mirror the surface of the terrain, forming ascending rows like a giant staircase. In a village on a mountainous plateau, houses are built next to one another, assuming the shape of an amphitheater. A narrow, upward-curving street often has steps cut out of the stone. Here and there, streets smoothly turn into tunnels, going through the ground floors of buildings and sometimes gradually making their way toward narrow arched bridges.

One of the primary concerns in building a house was the ability to defend it. Villages were designed to be inaccessible to enemies. As a rule, only one path led to a village, and it was protected and guarded by lookouts stationed in a watchtower. Some houses were built as towers and fortresses, reaching high into the sky. For safety purposes, such fortresses were built without windows. A large stone wall surrounded all household constructions, forming a single complex that was easy to defend. From the outside, all that was visible were blank walls and a tiny entrance. The back side of the structure typically faced an abyss or bordered a wall of rock. Some constructions were interconnected by underground walkways.

Villages still look quite similar to how they did in the past. Terraced fields hug the mountainsides, gardens grow among rocks, and sheep make their way along narrow paths above the abyss. While the setting can be beautiful and tranquil, life is hard high in the mountains, where the soil is so stony it is difficult to coax crops into growing. Still, many residents of these high-altitude settlements are in no hurry to leave their ancestral homes. Even suggesting that someone should leave the mountains for a new life on the plains can be taken as an offense.

FOLKTALES

Dagestani folklore reflects the strong dual influences of Islam and paganism. Islamic beliefs coexist and often merge with tales about hobgoblins, forest creatures, and a variety of demons. A story tells of a female demon meddling in the birth of a child. Demons of disease are believed to make people sick. Homes and cemeteries also have their share of resident demons. The Dagestani have plenty of rites and songs to protect themselves from evil spirits and to invite and welcome the more beneficial ones.

Tales, legends, and myths about unfortunate lovers, heroes, and fighters for independence teach young Dagestanis about codes of honor and dating rituals and encourage a better understanding of the history of their homeland.

Effendi Kapiev, an esteemed Dagestani writer of Lak origin, devoted his life to collecting folklore. At weddings and funerals, at fireplaces, and in workshops, he filled his notebooks with stories. Each page of his notebooks was filled with folk wisdom and the legends engraved on old daggers and somber gravestones.

LITERARY TRADITIONS

Between the 9th and 14th centuries, most Dagestani literary works were recorded in Arabic. Some works were produced in Persian, Azeri, and Turkish. The literature created in the languages of Dagestan's various ethnic groups first started appearing in the 14th century. Since the 19th century, many works have been written in Russian. Unfortunately, many key writings were lost because of the frequent changes to the alphabet.

"A poet is a peer of not only those living today, but those who have left and those who are to come to this earth," wrote Rasul Gamzatov, Dagestan's greatest poet. His works have been translated into many languages. Born in the tiny mountain village of Tsada, Gamzatov became one of the most prominent Soviet poets.

Other pillars of Dagestani literature include Kosta Hetagurov, Kyazim Mechiev, Suleiman Stalsky, and Gamzat Tsadasa. In Dagestan, literary artists are respected. Poems are cited in daily conversations and at celebrations, and some are turned into popular songs.

A modern Dagestani writer, Alisa Ganieva, has recently drawn international attention to her remote homeland. Ganieva's novels explore themes of modern life in Dagestan, including politics, religion, marriage, and the role of tradition. Her novels have been translated into several languages, including English, bringing an intimate view of Dagestan to readers around the world.

Alisa Ganieva won Russia's Debut Award in 2009 for her novella *Salaam, Dalgat!* The story follows a young man through one day in Makhachkala.

FINE ARTS

Painting did not come into its own in Dagestan until the 20th century. One of the first artists to introduce Dagestan to Western painting and techniques was Halilbek Musayasul. A Dagestani who was educated in Germany, Musayasul combined the traditions of the East and the West. Most of his symbolic, often grotesque, works were based on Dagestani themes.

His paintings have been exhibited in the best museums in Turkey, Germany, France, and the United States. The Metropolitan Museum of Art in New York City exhibits a cast of the artist's hands. Unable for dozens of years to return home from living abroad, Musayasul bequeathed all his works to his homeland. Although the artist's ashes are preserved in New Jersey, his works have now returned to the land of his ancestors.

The Avar State Music and Drama Theater is one of many performance halls in Makhachkala.

MUSIC AND THEATER

Like painting, theater had not been an integral part of Dagestani culture until the beginning of the 20th century. The first official theaters were founded as the offshoots of amateur companies. Theater has since become an increasingly important part of Dagestani culture. Directors stage both classical plays and pieces written in local languages by modern Dagestani playwrights.

The opening of the Russian Drama Theater and the Kumyk Theater of Music and Drama was followed by the founding of the Avar, Dargin, Lak, and Lezgin theaters. Today, theatrical presentations are staged at the State Opera and Ballet Theater as well as in smaller Azerbaijani, Nogay, or Tabasaran theaters. The capital also offers the Children's Theater. The Museum of the History of Dagestani Theaters attracts, in particular, those with an interest in the history of performance in the republic.

Musicians also have an important place in the art world of Dagestan. Important composers include Gotfried Hasanov and Shirvani Chalaev. In 1971, Chalaev wrote an opera set in Dagestan called *The Highlanders*. Another composer, Murad Kajlayev, set the words of Rasul Gamzatov to music to create the state anthem of the Republic of Dagestan.

INTERNET LINKS

https://dagartmuseum.dag.muzkult.ru/
Browse the collection of the Dagestan Museum of Fine Arts on its official website.

https://www.jozan.net/oriental-rugs-textiles/caucasian-rugs/daghestan-rugs/
This website displays a collection of traditional rugs and carpets from Dagestan.

https://www.kgou.org/post/alisa-ganieva-explores-complexities-culture-and-marriage-dagestan
Listen to an interview with Dagestani author Alisa Ganieva on KGOU's "World Views" program.

https://www.nationalgeographic.com/culture/2018/08/tightrope-walking-tradition-performance-dagestan-russia-children-youth/
Read about the daring feats of Dagestan's ropewalkers in this *National Geographic* article.

http://president.e-dag.ru/home/respublika/2013-03-24-22-53-33
Listen to Dagestan's anthem on the website of the president of Dagestan.

LEISURE

Physical activity is an important part of childhood in Dagestan. Many young people pursue training in dance or a sport.

WHEN PEOPLE IN DAGESTAN ARE looking to relax or socialize, they have a wide range of options to choose from. Athleticism is an important part of Dagestani culture, and many social events include physical challenges like dancing, ropewalking, and wrestling. Dagestan's beaches and thermal springs offer other popular settings for fun and relaxing outings.

No matter how busy they are, people strive to find time to spend with friends and family. While well-off city dwellers visit restaurants, home is the most popular gathering place for most Dagestanis. On Sundays, adults usually visit their parents. Guests are typically invited for dinner once or twice a week. People drop by even without an invitation, as guests are always welcome.

In Dagestan, like nearly everywhere in Russia, women have less free time than men. They also usually spend more time with children than men do. Besides sometimes working outside the home, they are responsible for the domestic upkeep of the household. Socializing with other women while performing their various daily tasks is a common activity in many Dagestani communities.

11

A 2014 study of the North Caucasus indicated that most Dagestani women spend their free time watching television, talking on the phone, visiting family, resting, and reading.

Leisure-seekers in Dagestan can visit the beaches along the Caspian Sea.

URBAN LEISURE

In cities, people can attend concerts and exhibitions and watch plays or movies. People generally do not go out alone. They bring along friends or family. Staying at home or socializing at home is also a common pastime.

Young urbanites use the latest apps and social media and play video games. They also go to nightclubs. Young women report using their free time to communicate on social media, go outdoors, and visit shopping malls and salons. Young men are more likely to spend time on sports activities and at gyms.

In summer, families spend a lot of time outdoors. City parks, especially at the seaside, are filled with people talking, playing with children, reading, or locked in a heated chess match. Crowds gather next to chessboards, cheering the players on. Children and teens ask their parents for money for amusement-park-style rides. People also go to the countryside, where some families have small country houses. Hiking and a variety of outdoor sports have become increasingly popular.

RURAL ATTRACTIONS

Villagers tend to have less free time than urban residents, and rural areas offer fewer opportunities for entertainment. As in cities, people spend a large share of their free time watching television. Most villages have a cultural or community center, called the "house of culture" during the Soviet era. The activities offered in the centers depend on the village's financial standing. Most cultural centers function as the local library and the movie theater. Those that have more funds at their disposal sometimes have billiard tables. It is mostly young men who gather there in the evenings. Young women commonly visit the center during the day. During late or nighttime hours, they arrive only in the company of an elder brother or cousin.

Dagestan has a rich supply of thermal springs, like this location in Izberbash. Spas and resorts have opened up to capitalize on these natural features.

The official count in 2016 calculated that there were 3,340 sports facilities in Dagestan, including sports halls, indoor and outdoor sports facilities, stadiums, swimming pools, and shooting galleries.

SOCIALIZING

A popular place for rural women of all ages to socialize and catch up is the public oven or the local water source. While talking there, they never put their heavy water jugs on the ground, as they do not want to be perceived by other villagers as being lazy and gossipy.

Rural men spend virtually all their free time on the godekan. A centrally located square, the godekan has many functions. First of all, it is where men develop socially, learning the qualities of namus and yag'. It is also a place where the older and younger generations meet. Elders gather there, and it is the place where important community decisions are made. The elders, sitting on benches, watch young men playing sports. Locals also come to the godekan to meet friends, share news, get advice, play games, or sell goods. Travelers come to the square to find lodging. A godekan, however, is a men's club where women are not welcome.

In cities, a godekan does not exist. Nonetheless, men born in rural areas attempt to create godekan-like enclaves in city parks. Old men sitting on benches try to engage in conversations with passersby or give advice to the young. Many townsfolk, however, find such behavior unusual.

MUSIC

Many Dagestanis love singing. They honor and praise their most talented singers. People sing at work, in their free time, and during celebrations. During winter, when the harvest is over, some villages host singing contests, which attract the best singers in the area. Previously, only men were allowed to take part in these contests, but today, women also participate. Folk songs—both religious and secular—were often performed as dialogues. A man would start, and a male choir would join in, repeating the refrain. Then, a woman would answer the first singer, after which other women would pick up the tune. People sing without accompaniment or to the strains of the *buben* (BOO-ben), *chungur* (choon-GOOR), *tanbur* (tahn-BOOR), *zurna*, and *svirel* (svee-REHL)—the main Dagestani percussion, string, and wind instruments

ATHLETICS

Dagestanis joke that they rank first in the number of Olympic medals any nation has won in respect to the total population. Dagestani freestyle wrestlers and boxers regularly secure Olympic medals. Wrestling in Dagestan has historic roots. The resistance to the various invasions that have shaken the region fostered the development of martial arts and wrestling. Since early childhood, the typical Dagestani boy is brought up to be a defender. The stress placed on strength and physical prowess has contributed to the development of excellent wrestling schools. No feast in Dagestan is celebrated without a wrestling competition, both among men and boys. In addition, Dagestani sportsmen have attained high international rankings in the martial arts, pistol shooting, and archery. In a land where vigor is highly prized, successful and esteemed athletes have become heroes. The republic takes pride in athletes of Dagestani origin who have won medals in the Olympic Games while representing Russia.

At the 2016 Summer Olympics, 24 athletes from Dagestan competed for the Russian Federation and other countries.

Wrestling schools and gyms are found throughout Dagestan. The history of Dagestanis as fierce warriors has continued in the legacy of its athletes.

It is not only tourists who take part in the extreme outdoor sports made possible by Dagestan's mountainous terrain. Locals also join in the fun. In summer, Dagestan's waterfalls appeal to those looking for a place to swim in refreshing mountain water. Frozen waterfalls in winter fascinate a more adventurous crew.

In the Khunzakhsky District of Dagestan, a yearly ice climbing festival draws in visitors and locals alike. The Dagestan Open Ice Climbing Competition tests the strength and skill of athletes from across Russia. In February 2020, the event took place at the Matlas Waterfalls. It attracted 85 participants, who competed as teams and individuals for awards.

Climbers ascend a solid waterfall in Dagestan with the help of ice picks and special boots at the 2016 Ice Climbing Competition.

CHEERING ON KHABIB

In Dagestan, there is a strong sense of pride in local athletes. All of Dagestan seems to cheer on its greatest athletes in international competitions, especially when it comes to Khabib Nurmagomedov. Nurmagomedov electrified Dagestan and the world as the reigning Ultimate Fighting Championship (UFC) Lightweight Champion in 2017, 2018, and 2019. Khabib's global reputation as a determined and accomplished fighter has also sparked a wide interest in his homeland.

As a Dagestani champion, Khabib Nurmagomedov has shown great pride in where he comes from. He can be recognized at international competitions, like this one in 2019, by the *papakha* he wears.

INTERNET LINKS

http://khabib.com/en/
The official website of Khabib Nurmagomedov, Dagestan's celebrated mixed martial artist, documents his latest training, competitions, and victories.

https://www.theguardian.com/world/gallery/2016/feb/15/climbing-a-frozen-waterfall-in-dagestan
The *Guardian* offers a photo gallery from the 2016 Ice Climbing Festival in Dagestan.

FESTIVALS

Dagestani dancers in traditional dress
celebrate Russia Day in 2018

12

Makhachkala
has hosted
"Highlanders," an
International Festival
of Folklore and
Traditional Culture,
every summer
since 2004.

DAGESTAN'S HOLIDAYS CAN BE sorted into different categories based on their origins. Islamic holidays are celebrated by the more than 90 percent of the Dagestani people who are Muslim. Seasonal and cultural holidays have roots in the ancient past, agricultural cycle, and diverse ethnic makeup of life in Dagestan. Secular holidays point to Dagestan's ties to Russia and its Soviet past.

Some Dagestani festivals draw together Islamic and folk traditions with Russian and Soviet celebrations. Many holiday customs and practices even reflect ancient Eastern religions. Islamic holidays are celebrated according to the Islamic calendar, and their dates shift each year. On Islamic holidays, believers go to the mosque for public prayer and a sermon.

Folk holidays can be divided into spring, summer, and fall celebrations. Spring holidays symbolize the preparation prior to the planting season and provide the last chance to relax before the hard work begins. Spring and summer holidays unite the entire village community and often bear romantic or sentimental associations. The beauty of nature and the inviting temperatures of the summer months are conducive to entertainment, games, and sports competitions. In the fall, Dagestanis celebrate the harvest with family and neighbors. Winter is the time to rest after the long hours of labor. It is the time for family celebrations and quiet evenings with friends and relatives.

ISLAMIC HOLIDAYS

JUMA   The Juma day of Friday is a weekly Islamic holiday, equivalent to the Sabbath day of Sunday for Christians and Saturday for Jews. On Friday, Muslims gather in a mosque for the special prayer and sermon. The Prophet Muhammad chose that specific day as "the light of Islam" started spreading on a Friday. According to Islamic belief, a Friday will be the day the dead are resurrected. Although Friday is a work day in the republic, religious Dagestanis dress up, cook special food, and visit relatives and friends nonetheless.

KURBAN BAIRAM   Kurban Bairam (in Turkic), or Eid al-Adha (in Arabic), is a day honoring sacrifice to God. It is one of the most honored holidays for Dagestani Muslims. There are special and regular sacrifices. A special sacrifice may be made to fulfil a vow—perhaps in asking for a son—or as a public sign of

A man chooses a ram to be sacrificed for Kurban Bairam. The holiday usually takes place at the end of July or beginning of August.

repentance for sins. To demonstrate repentance, the entire body of a sacrificial animal is given to the poor. In a regular sacrifice, one-third of the meat goes to the family offering the sacrifice, and the rest is given to the poor.

Not only the celebration itself but also the process of preparing for it are intricate and ceremonial. A special service to God takes place in the mosques. People cook elaborate meals, consisting particularly of meat dishes; dress in their best clothes; and visit their family and friends to offer them presents. People also visit the graves of their ancestors and give alms. More and more, Kurban Bairam is celebrated by a growing circle of people.

MAVLID   The celebration of Mavlid, the Prophet Muhammad's birthday, became widespread in Dagestan during the 1950s. Since no one knows the exact day when he was born, some Muslims celebrate his birthday throughout the month of Rabi ul-avval.

Mullahs, familiar with the ceremony, stay quite busy during the month, as they are invited every day to visit different families. A mullah sings rhymes about the birth and life of Muhammad and about his glorious deeds. Every four lines, the group repeats a refrain.

The final part of the ceremony is *zikr*, where a soloist is accompanied by the group, singing a thousand times the words *La ilaha illallah*, meaning "There is no other God than Allah." People sit in a circle, rocking their heads left and right, sometimes reaching a trancelike state, which they come out of with the help of the mullah.

URAZA BAIRAM   Uraza Bairam, or Eid al-Fitr in Arabic, celebrates the end of a 30-day period of fasting called Ramadan. It typically brings more joy than Kurban Bairam because it celebrates the end of a challenging period in which Muslims cannot eat or drink from sunrise to sunset. The Uraza Bairam ceremony consists of a special public prayer followed by a meal that extends over several hours. On Uraza Bairam, people visit their family and friends and exchange gifts. Dressed festively, people take walks, visit the graves of their ancestors, and give alms to the poor.

FOLK HOLIDAYS

Navruz has much in common with ancient pagan rituals once performed by the local populations.

NAVRUZ   The vernal equinox, around March 21, is celebrated by most Dagestanis as Navruz, or the Islamic New Year. Navruz (also known as Nowruz) is a celebration of life in which warmth and light win out over the forces of evil and the chill of the winter.

Dagestanis start preparing for Navruz well in advance. Women cook flour cereal, enough for several days, as it is commonly believed that the longer the cereal lasts, the longer prosperity will stay in the house. Women also bake special bread in the shape of animals, birds, or people. This bread is given as a gift to the friends and relatives who come to visit the family in the evening. The villagers gather to eat and have fun. Girls tell fortunes, and young men compete in wrestling. The winner will have good luck in the new year.

Late at night, each family lights a fire in the yard. In darkness, the village, seen from afar, looks like a gigantic torch. Boys shoot little clay balls with burning twigs inside them. The sound of clay balls crackling in flight is believed to scare off evil spirits. People entertain themselves by jumping over fires that are thought to help spring gain its force. All sorrow and grief burn in the fire, and people step into the new year cleansed of evil and full of renewed hope. The ashes and coals from Navruz fires are collected and kept throughout the next year as a form of protection.

THE FIRST FURROW   The celebration of the first furrow dates back to ancient times. Today, it is a sophisticated ceremony, performed in various ways by different ethnic groups. The main idea of the rite, however, is common to all. On the day of the vernal equinox, rural residents come to the fields to make the first furrows. A ritual announces the beginning of the planting season and aims to secure an abundant harvest. Muslim ethnic groups invite mullahs to read prayers. The celebration continues with horseback riding, wrestling, and stone throwing.

DAY OF FLOWERS   The Day of Flowers is one of the year's most beautiful events. Previously it was celebrated only on Mount Chapar-Suv, where the Ahtyns concluded peace talks with their neighbors. The holiday has since been

used to commemorate peace and even to appease enemies. It is celebrated on all mountains and hillsides that are dotted with wildflowers.

The young especially look forward to the Day of Flowers because it gives them a chance to meet someone from a different village and to make a connection that might potentially lead to marriage. Young men chosen by the elders compete in a 6-mile (10 km) race. They run up a hill or mountain, starting fires along the way. At night, dancing and singing, young Dagestanis carry torches up the hill to watch the sunrise from the mountaintop. They go back to their villages at noon, where they are greeted by the elders, who do not take part in the celebration. The young give them flowers, after which they return to their homes.

CHERRY DAY The cherries start to ripen in mid-June in Dagestan. Then, the word *karu* (kah-ROO), meaning "cherry," starts traveling from one aoul

Wildflowers from alpine meadows are collected to celebrate the Day of Flowers.

Dagestan's flag and coat of arms are often displayed at state holidays and on official buildings. The flag is made up of three equal and horizontal bands of color. A green band is a sign of life and a reference to the traditional color of Islam. A blue band represents water and the importance of the Caspian Sea. A red band stands for democracy and the courage of the Dagestani people.

Dagestan's state emblem, or coat of arms, features a golden eagle. Eagles are an important symbol in Dagestan. They represent strength, pride, courage, and freedom. A round, golden sun shines above the eagle's head as a sign of light and abundance. Images of snow-capped mountains, a plain, and the sea appear below the eagle. A handshake at the bottom of the emblem stands for the cooperation and hospitality of Dagestan's people.

Knowledge Day is celebrated in Russia to mark the beginning of the school year in September. Teachers and students come together for songs, speeches, and introductions. The students usually present their teachers with flowers.

to another. Villagers gather in shady gardens to savor the first cherries of the year. People dance, sing, and compete in horseback riding contests.

SECULAR HOLIDAYS

CONSTITUTION DAY The day the second constitution of Dagestan was adopted (July 26, 2003) is widely celebrated in the republic's urban areas. City residents dress up in traditional costumes and dance, play games, or stroll in the central streets. At night, fireworks illuminate the sky, and thousands of balloons in the colors of the Dagestani flag soar into the air and out of sight.

NEW YEAR New Year's Day is one of the republic's most popular holidays. Preparation for the new year starts well in advance. Houses and streets are decorated with garlands and toys. Everyone buys New Year's presents and sends greeting cards to friends and family.

On December 31, Dagestanis part with the old year and leave their sorrows in the past. Guests come in the evening and take seats at a table laden with food and drink. When the clock strikes 12 at midnight, everyone makes a wish, gets up from his or her seat, clinks glasses, and says, "New Year, New Happiness!" Eating and dancing then continue late into the night.

During the Soviet era, Dagestanis started celebrating the New Year, International Women's Day (March 8), Victory Day (May 9) to mark the end of World War II, Labor Day (May 1), and the Socialist Revolution Day (November 7). The New Year is the most celebrated of the surviving Soviet holidays.

Veterans celebrate Victory Day in 2020, which marked the 75th anniversary of Russia's victory over Nazi Germany.

INTERNET LINKS

https://www.britannica.com/topic/Eid-al-Adha
Encyclopedia Britannica offers an entry on Eid al-Adha, also called Kurban Bairam in Dagestan.

https://www.britannica.com/topic/Eid-al-Fitr
Encyclopedia Britannica provides information about the Islamic festival Eid al-Fitr, also called Uraza Bairam in Dagestan.

https://www.newsweek.com/what-may-ninth-and-why-it-so-important-russia-605639
This article from *Newsweek* explains the significance of Victory Day in Russia.

FOOD

A woman in Dagestan bakes flatbread in a hand-built oven. Wheat, corn flour, and rye are often used in Dagestani breads.

13

DAGESTAN'S REGIONAL CUISINE IS rooted in the history and geography of the region. The mountainous terrain and lowland pastures have made it possible for Dagestani shepherds to raise sheep, cattle, and other livestock for centuries. As a result, meat and dairy feature heavily in regional dishes. Grains, fruits, and vegetables suited to the environment have been grown on Dagestan's limited arable land. These crops have also become fundamental ingredients. Many Dagestanis use traditional recipes for bread, soup, cereals, meat, and dairy dishes that take advantage of local food availability.

Modern Dagestani food combines the thousand-year-old cooking traditions of indigenous ethnic groups with outside culinary influences. The Nogays and Kumyks gave Dagestani cuisine a Mongolian touch; the Tats shared a Persian flavor. The remarkably diverse Azeri cuisine added variety to Dagestani food as well. The Russians, Ukrainians, and Belarusians brought, in turn, their own recipes and introduced potatoes,

Dagestanis increase nutrient content by waiting until grains have begun to sprout before grinding them into flour.

Before an important meal, a *tamada*—a feast leader and toastmaster—is chosen to preside over the event.

cabbage, and tomatoes. Developments during the Soviet era enriched Dagestani cuisine with candies, salads, macaroni, and canned and convenience foods. In addition, people acquired new means of storing food as well as new types of kitchen utensils and appliances.

Religion has also shaped the republic's attitude toward food. Neither Muslims nor Jews eat pork. Herds of sheep and cattle grazing on hillsides and in the mountains provide meat. Lamb and mutton are the preferred choices of Dagestani Muslims and Jews, while Christians have no dietary restrictions.

SHARING MEALS

Mealtimes in Dagestan are social events. Food and drink seem to be secondary— it is the people that matter most. Dagestanis eat three times a day. Breakfast is a quick, light meal eaten early in the morning. Working people have lunch either at a cafeteria or drop by their home during their lunch break. Those with a free schedule have lunch somewhere between 1 p.m. and 3 p.m. Later, the family gathers for dinner, the main meal of the day.

A Dagestani meal consists of one course and a beverage. Because there is only one major dish, plates are usually filled with it. People are brought up from an early age to be reserved in eating. This tradition is partly shaped by the general lack of time. Women work hard throughout the day at their various duties and domestic chores and do not have the time to prepare several courses.

Certain table manners are important to know before visiting a Dagestani family. Because Dagestanis love guests, an outsider is offered food as soon as he or she enters the house. Dagestanis view the serving of guests as an honor. The elder members of the family usually take their seats first and are served first as well. Guests are seated according to their age and relative status. The head of the family begins the meal. In villages, family members sometimes eat from a large central dish. At the table, people try to be considerate.

Before each sip of an alcoholic drink, Dagestanis clink glasses and pronounce a long and often poetic toast. Making a toast is an art form, and people compete in the eloquence of their speeches. They raise glasses to love, health, happiness, and good luck and address their wishes to guests, parents, friends, or children. The Aguls are the only Dagestani ethnic group who do not offer toasts at

Food and drink have always been an important ingredient in Dagestani festivals and holidays. More recently, the region's culinary achievements became a primary reason for one celebration. In 2016, the first Mountain Tea Festival was held in the village of Sogratl, Dagestan. The event was designed to showcase regional black and herbal tea varieties. Dagestani cuisine also received a spotlight. In addition to sampling various teas and ethnic delicacies, participants could learn how to prepare traditional dishes. A second festival followed in 2017 against the breathtaking backdrop of the Sulak Canyon. The event was organized by Dagestan's Ministry for Tourism and Folk Art Crafts.

feasts. Drinking in the company of elderly people, a young person can empty their glass only after being asked repeatedly to do so. Important to Dagestani society is the attitude toward drunkenness and imbibing large amounts of alcohol. A simple unspoken rule prevails: As soon as a person feels they may have had too much to drink, he or she should quietly leave the table. Tea is also an important beverage in Dagestan.

DIVERSE DUMPLINGS

Hinkal (heen-KAHL), sometimes spelled *khinkal*, is a plain dumpling with no filling. It is the most popular Dagestani dish with a wide variety of forms and tastes. Hinkal can differ in the flour used to make the dough, the shape of the dumplings, the type of meat that accompanies them, and the sauce drizzled over them or served on the side. Although hinkal is made all over Dagestan, experienced gourmets can tell the origin or home affiliation of the cook after a few bites.

Dumplings of all imaginable shapes and sizes are made of wheat, rye, barley, bean, or corn flour. Corn-flour hinkal is especially prevalent in the cuisines of Dagestanis, Chechens, and Kumyks. In Archib, however, where corn does not grow, corn-flour hinkal with fresh milk is considered a delicacy and is served only on special occasions.

Among most ethnic groups, hinkal is served with garlic sauce and any of a number of dairy products: yogurt, sour milk, sour cream, butter, or cheese. Many people eat hinkal with fresh or dried meat or sausage. Avars, Dargins, and Agouls often dress hinkal with mutton fat. Kumyks serve hinkal with tomatoes and nuts, while Tats tend to prefer theirs with generous helpings of vegetables and fruit. Avari hinkal sometimes comes with *urbech*, a seasoning made either of slightly fried, ground flaxseeds mixed with butter and honey or of ground nuts

Kurze, seen here, and hinkal are served in different regional styles and come in a variety of shapes and sizes.

mixed with fresh or dried apricots.

Finally, hinkal can be presented in many different ways. Some cooks leave dumplings floating in a soup, while others serve them separately on a plate with a cup of broth accompanying them.

Filled dumplings, referred to as *kurze* (koor-ZEH), *kazan borek* (ka-ZAHN boh-REHK), *pelmeni*, and *vareniki*, should not be confused with hinkal, which are dumplings without filling. Meat and cottage cheese are popular dumpling fillings. Russian pelmeni are exclusively stuffed with meat. Dargin dumplings are filled with poultry, spring onion, eggs, pumpkin, potatoes, carrots, or fresh and dried apricots. Tsakhours make a special filling by mixing milk with eggs and nettles with nuts. Kumyk cuisine features dumplings filled with pumpkin, nettles, or liver. Ukrainians usually fill their vareniki with potatoes, cottage cheese, or cherries.

SAVORY PIES

Pies such as *chudu* (choo-DOO), *burkiv* (boor-KEEV), and *pirogi* are a mainstay of Dagestani cuisine. Like dumplings, pies can differ in size and filling. The most popular fillings are meat and cottage cheese, followed by nettles and eggs. In addition, Archins serve pies with mutton fat or liver. Avars also eat them with mutton fat, while Kumyks prefer liver or pumpkin. Laks make pies with pumpkin, sorrel, and goosefoot, a type of plant. Dargin pies come with an assortment of fillings. Pumpkin, potatoes, spring onion, carrots, and fresh and dried apricots are just some of the fruits and vegetables found tucked inside. Russians, Ukrainians, and Belarusians bake mushroom, fish, apple, plum, and cherry pies.

ETHNIC RECIPES

Over the years, the differences and distinctions among the cuisines of Dagestan's ethnic groups have slowly begun to erode. This development is especially apparent in the cities, where people have a wide assortment of food at their disposal in grocery stores and at markets.

In addition, the republic's urban centers tend to draw a more diverse blend of people; this contributes to the interchange and evolution of culinary practices. The influence of Russian cuisine has been particularly strong, and Russian dishes are now part of most people's daily diets. Despite the commonality in much modern Dagestani cooking, people still retain their traditional preferences and signature dishes.

INDIGENOUS PEOPLES AND THE TATS   Among the Tats and the region's original settlers, daily foods include hinkal and various pies, soups, and cereals. Lamb is the meat of choice, and mutton fat is added to many dishes. Some village residents dry meat and sausage for winter. Meat dishes, such as *shashlyk* (grilled lamb), *dolma* (grape leaves stuffed with meat and rice), and pilaf (a blend of rice and meat) are at the heart of Tat cuisine. The traditional sheep's milk cheese *brynza* (BRYN-zah) is also popular. A variety of seasonings is used: pepper, caraway seeds, thyme, ground walnuts, barberries, and vinegar. Tats are renowned for their spices, pickles, marinades, and especially their hot pickled peppers.

Tea is a favorite Tat beverage, including Kalmyk salty tea, as well as *bouza* (boo-ZAH) and *ayran* (ahi-RAHN). Creamy drinks are made from different types of yogurt. The Dargins from Kaitag make *musti*, a boiled muscat wine, and also brew raisin beer. Tats brew a distinctive liquor that is similar to ouzo or *araki*, a licorice-flavored liqueur.

KUMYKS Kumyk specialties include rice-, corn-, or wheat-flour cereal called *chilav* (chee-LAHV) and *sorpa* (sohr-PAH), or soup, made with beans, rice, noodles, or nettles. Kumyks also make *kuvurma*, a meat sauce, and *kuimak*, whipped eggs. Like other peoples of the Caucasus, Kumyks love hinkal, kurze, chudu, dolma, shashlyk, and pilaf. Kumyk desserts include halva, pancakes, and jams. Favorite drinks are Kalmyk salty tea, coffee, and cocoa, which came from the West.

NOGAYS Nogays are famous for *kouvyrdak* (koo-vyr-DAHK), or fried meat with onions; a meat-and-noodle dish called *beshbarmak* (besh-bahr-MAHK); *balyk* (bah-LYK) *sorpa*, or fish soup; and the sausages *kazy* and *toltyrma* (tohl-tyr-MAH). Nogays also love shashlyk, pies, and eggs. Nogay cuisine is notable for its wide array of beverages. *Nogay shai* (tea), *koumiss* (mare's milk), *suv* (sherbet), and yogurt are commonly served at Nogay tables.

MOUNTAIN JEWS The Mountain Jews are known for their fish, lamb, and chicken dishes, which are generally served with rice and vegetables. Fish is eaten dried, pickled, smoked, fried, boiled, or stuffed. The Mountain Jews traditionally grew and picked various greens and seasoned food with plums, cherry plums, sloes, onions, and garlic. Specialties are a meat-and-vegetable blend called *bugleme* (boog-leh-MEH), a meat-and-onion stew coated with eggs called *khoe-gusht* (hoheh-GOOSHT), a type of dolma called *yapragy* (yah-prah-GY), hinkal, and pilaf. The food of Mountain Jews has been influenced by other regional cuisines, most notably Iranian and Azeri cuisines.

SLAVS The food of Dagestani Russians, Ukrainians, and Belarusians has been strongly influenced by local and native Dagestani cuisine. Slavs in Dagestan cook kurze, dolma, shashlyk, hinkal, and other local specialties. Traditional Slavic dishes are *borsch*, or red beet soup; pelmeni, or meat dumplings; pancakes; and *golubtsy*, or cabbage leaves stuffed with meat and rice. Potatoes, noodles, and cereals are common side dishes that remain popular as well.

MODERN DINING

Meat, dairy, and flour continue to form the foundation of many meals among Dagestan's diverse ethnic groups. In the capital city of Makhachkala, restaurants and cafés offer generous servings of regional foods. Traditional dishes from across the republic can be found there alongside creative twists on classic meals.

Fishing has influenced Dagestani cuisine since ancient times. Locals in Derbent prepare recipes with Caspian *kutum*, a species of fish native to the Caspian Sea.

INTERNET LINKS

http://www.eng.kavkaz-uzel.eu/articles/36474/
This article covers the details of the first Mountain Tea Festival in Dagestan.

http://www.ethnotraveler.com/2014/01/drink-plenty-of-tea-and-bathe-once-a-week/
Read a traveler's account of meals and tea enjoyed with mountain residents of southern Dagestan.

https://foodperestroika.com/2019/03/04/khinkal-dagestans-national-dish/
This page provides an excellent introduction to hinkal in Dagestan, with images and descriptions of its many ethnic varieties.

CHUDU

2 cups dry farmer's cheese
3 medium potatoes, peeled and boiled
   until tender
¼ teaspoon baking soda
4 cups all-purpose flour

1 cup (0.2 liters) water
salt
sugar
butter

Make the dough: Measure flour into a large bowl, and add a pinch of salt.
Using your hands, mix in up to 1 cup of water until a soft, smooth dough forms.
Put the dough aside to rest in the bowl.

Make the filling: Grate the boiled potatoes into a large bowl.
Add farmer's cheese, baking soda, a pinch of salt, and a pinch of sugar, and mix together well.
Form the mixture into 3-inch (7.5 centimeter) balls.

Assemble the chudu: Turn the dough out onto a lightly floured surface.
Divide the dough into 12 pieces with a knife, and roll each piece into a ball.
Using a rolling pin, roll each ball of dough into a flat disc, about 5 inches (13 cm) wide.
Place a ball of filling into the center of each disc. Pull the dough up and around the filling, and gather at the top to create a pouch. Press tightly to seal the pouch shut, then cut off any excess dough at the top.
Turn the pouch seal-side down, and roll out the filled ball into a large flat disc, about 0.5 inch (1.25 cm) thick.

Cook the chudu: Place a dry skillet over high heat.
Place one chudu at a time on the skillet, cooking 1—2 minutes on each side. As the chudu puffs up, pop any bubbles with a fork or knife.
Remove from the skillet, and brush with butter. Stack the cooked chudu on a plate.
Serve hot with the stack cut into six slices.

APRICOT PORRIDGE WITH FLAXSEED URBECH

1½ cups flaxseeds
2 teaspoons honey
pinch of salt
2 tablespoons water
4 cups fresh, canned, or frozen
    apricots (or peaches)
½ tablespoon wheat flour

For the urbech: Grind flaxseeds with a coffee grinder, food processor, or mortar and pestle until powdered.
Add honey, salt, and water to the powdered seeds, and mix well.
Transfer paste to a jar. After using, store the jar in the refrigerator.

For the porridge: Chop apricots or peaches, and remove the pits.
Blend the fruit in a blender or food processor.
Transfer the fruit to a medium-size saucepan.
Cook over medium heat, stirring constantly until it comes to a boil.
Add flour, then cook on low heat for five minutes.
Ladle cooked porridge into bowls. Top with a spoonful of urbech and serve.

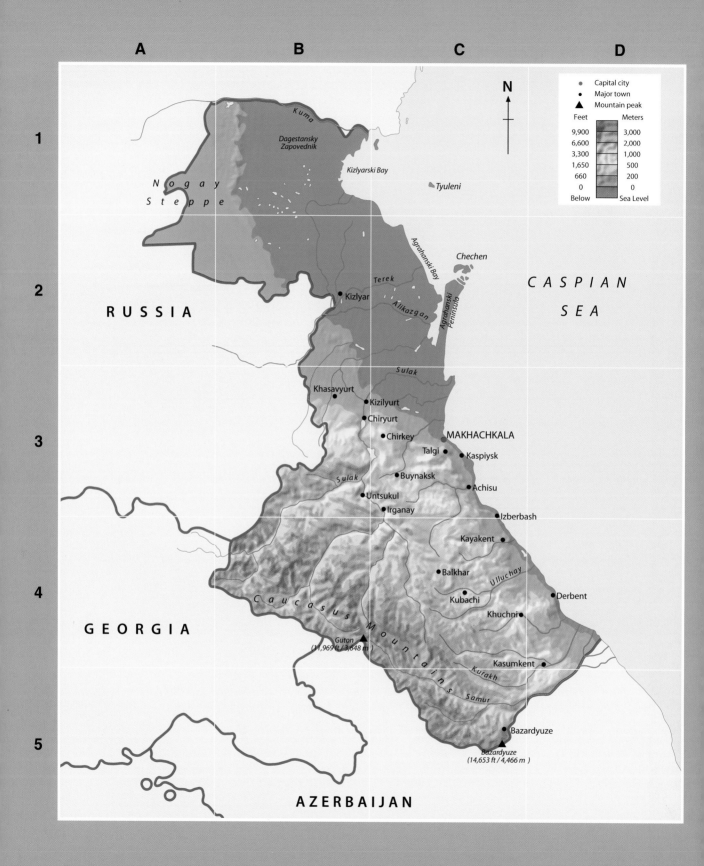

MAP OF DAGESTAN

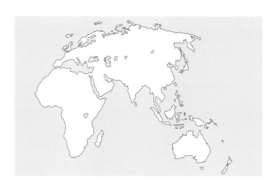

ECONOMIC DAGESTAN

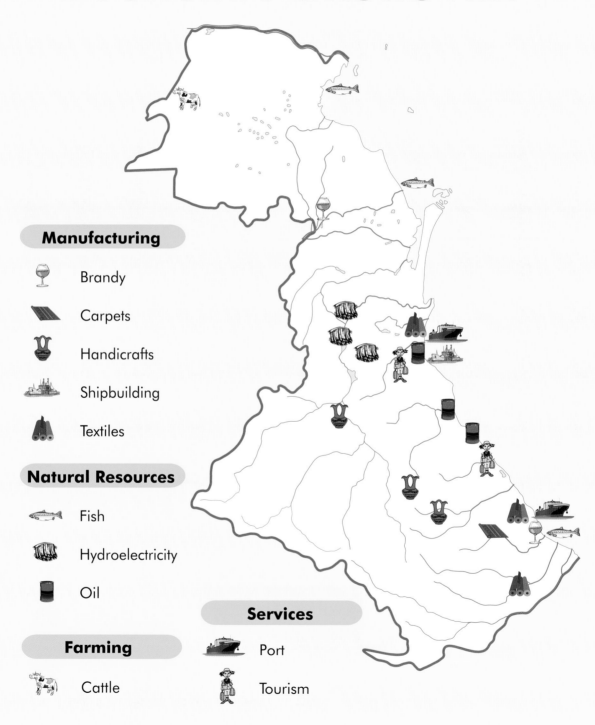

Manufacturing

- Brandy
- Carpets
- Handicrafts
- Shipbuilding
- Textiles

Natural Resources

- Fish
- Hydroelectricity
- Oil

Farming

- Cattle

Services

- Port
- Tourism

ABOUT THE ECONOMY

All figures are 2017 estimates unless otherwise noted.

OVERVIEW

When the USSR collapsed, the new Republic of Dagestan had to figure out how to survive outside the Soviet framework that had supplied most of the demand and support for Dagestani industry. Dagestan's economy remains closely connected to that of Russia and has shrunk and grown more or less in tandem with it since 1991. Manufacturing of shipped goods and power, gas, and water distribution account for most of Dagestan's gross regional product (GRP).

LAND AREA

19,400 square miles (50,300 square km), with 336 miles (540 km) of coastline; arable land makes up 12 percent of the total area

CURRENCY

1 Russia ruble (RUB) = 100 kopeks
USD 1 = RUB 73.46 (August 2020)
notes: 50, 100, 200, 500, 1000, 2000, 5000 rubles
coins minted: 1, 2, 5, 10 rubles

NATURAL RESOURCES

oil, natural gas, coal, water

AGRICULTURAL PRODUCTS

fish, fruit, vegetables, meat

INDUSTRIAL PRODUCTS/ACTIVITY

chemicals, construction, food products (including wine and brandy), glass, hydroelectric power, large-scale engineering, machinery and tools, shipbuilding, textiles, traditional handicrafts

CULTURAL DAGESTAN

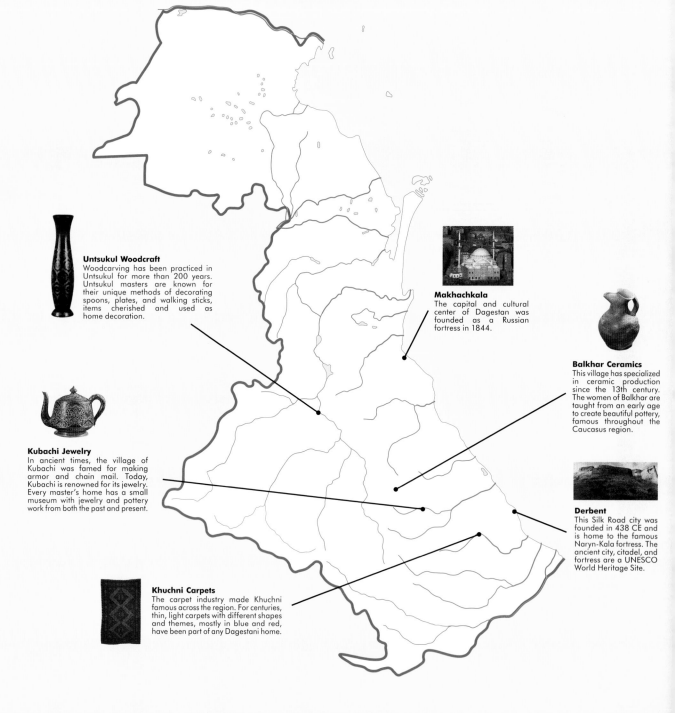

Untsukul Woodcraft
Woodcarving has been practiced in Untsukul for more than 200 years. Untsukul masters are known for their unique methods of decorating spoons, plates, and walking sticks, items cherished and used as home decoration.

Makhachkala
The capital and cultural center of Dagestan was founded as a Russian fortress in 1844.

Balkhar Ceramics
This village has specialized in ceramic production since the 13th century. The women of Balkhar are taught from an early age to create beautiful pottery, famous throughout the Caucasus region.

Kubachi Jewelry
In ancient times, the village of Kubachi was famed for making armor and chain mail. Today, Kubachi is renowned for its jewelry. Every master's home has a small museum with jewelry and pottery work from both the past and present.

Derbent
This Silk Road city was founded in 438 CE and is home to the famous Naryn-Kala fortress. The ancient city, citadel, and fortress are a UNESCO World Heritage Site.

Khuchni Carpets
The carpet industry made Khuchni famous across the region. For centuries, thin, light carpets with different shapes and themes, mostly in blue and red, have been part of any Dagestani home.

ABOUT THE CULTURE

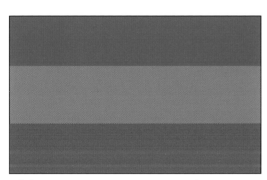

All figures are 2017 estimates unless otherwise noted.

OFFICIAL NAME
Republic of Dagestan

POLITICAL STATUS
Constituent Unit of the Russian Federation

FLAG
three horizontal bands in green, blue, and red

COAT OF ARMS
round, white heraldic shield with a golden eagle in the middle and the sun above; the upper part of the shield has a gold border; the lower part, bordered in blue on the left and in red on the right, shows snowy mountain peaks, a plain, the sea, and a handshake bounded by a green heraldic band with the words "Republic of Dagestan"

CAPITAL
Makhachkala

OTHER CITIES
Derbent, Buynaksk, Izberbash, Kaspiysk, Khasavyurt, Kizilyurt, Kizlyar

POPULATION
3,085,700 (2019)

ETHNIC GROUPS
Avars 29.4 percent; Dargins 16.9 percent; Kumyks 14.9 percent; Lezgins 13.3 percent; Laks 5.6 percent; Azeris 4.5 percent; Tabasarans 4.1 percent; Russians 3.6 percent; Chechens 3.2 percent; Nogay 1.4 percent; Rutuls 1 percent; Aguls 1 percent; Tsakhurs 0.3 percent

RELIGIONS
Islam (more than 90 percent Sunni Muslims), Christianity, Judaism

LANGUAGES
Russian and 14 indigenous languages are the official languages of Dagestan. In addition, there are more than 30 local languages, including Avar, Dargin, Kumyk, Lezgin, Lak, Azeri, and Tabasaran.

FESTIVALS AND HOLIDAYS
Kurban Bairam, Uraza Bairam, Navruz, International Women's Day (March 8), Victory Day (May 9), Constitution Day (July 26)

LEADERS IN THE ARTS
Rasul Gamzatov (poet), Alisa Ganieva (writer), Halilbek Musayasul (painter)

TIME
Greenwich Mean Time plus three hours (GMT + 03:00)

TIMELINE

IN DAGESTAN	IN THE WORLD
First millennium BCE	
Caucasian Albania, the first big state in the eastern Caucasus, emerges.	
Eighth century BCE	
There is evidence of a settlement in Derbent from this time.	**116–117 CE**
	The Roman Empire reaches its greatest extent, under Emperor Trajan.
Third century CE	
Sasanids of Persia invade the southern part of what is now Dagestan.	
Fourth century	
Huns capture the coastline to the north of Derbent.	
Fifth century	**600 CE**
Sizable cities emerge, most notable Derbent (438 CE), Semender, and Kubachi.	The height of the Maya civilization is reached.
664–914	
Dagestan is subject to repeated invasions by the Arabs.	**1000**
11th century	The Chinese perfect gunpowder and begin to use it in warfare.
Seljuk Turks capture what is now Azerbaijan and part of Dagestan.	
1220	
Dagestan is invaded by the Mongols.	**1530**
mid-1500s	The beginning of the transatlantic slave trade is organized by the Portuguese in Africa.
Russians enter the Caucasus; the first serious interactions between Dagestani tribes and Russians begin.	**1558–1603**
	The reign of Elizabeth I of England occurs.
	1620
	The Pilgrims sail the *Mayflower* to America.
1722	**1776**
Peter the Great invades Persia and the eastern Caucasus.	The U.S. Declaration of Independence is written.
	1789–1799
1813	The French Revolution takes place.
The Russians and Persians sign the Gulistan Peace Treaty. Persia cedes the khanates along the Caspian Sea to Russia.	

IN DAGESTAN	IN THE WORLD
1817–1864 The Caucasian War is fought between the northern Caucasian mountain tribes and Russia.	**1861** The American Civil War begins. **1914** World War I begins.
1917 A revolution in Russia takes place.	
1921 The Autonomous Republic of Dagestan is established by the Bolshevik government.	**1939** World War II begins.
	1957 The Russians launch *Sputnik*.
1991 Dagestan declares itself a sovereign republic.	**1991** The breakup of the Soviet Union takes place.
1994–1996 The first Chechen War is fought.	
1999–2009 The second Chechen War is fought. Chechen militants invade Dagestan in an attempt to establish a Muslim state.	**2001** Terrorists crash planes in New York, Washington, D.C., and Pennsylvania.
2009 Interior minister Adilgerei Magomedtagirov is assassinated.	**2003** The Iraq War begins.
2011 Dagestan is named the most dangerous place in Europe.	**2011** The United States officially declares an end to the war in Iraq.
	2016 Donald Trump is elected president of the United States.
2018 Vladimir Vasilyev is confirmed as Head of the Government of the Republic of Dagestan.	
2020 Dagestan's government is accused of falsifying COVID-19 data.	**2019** The COVID-19 outbreak begins in Wuhan Province, China.

GLOSSARY

ajam
An alphabet based on Arabic script.

aoul
A village.

chaban
A shepherd.

dzhigit
A rider; figuratively, it means a deft, brave man.

farmingo
A trick performed by ropewalkers.

gazavat
In Islam, armed defense or struggle against the unfaithful.

godekan
A village square, usually with a mosque; the center of communication and socializing for men living in rural areas.

hajj
A journey to Mecca for religious purposes that all Muslims try to make at least once in their lifetime.

jamaat
A rural community.

lezginka
A famous Dagestani dance.

madrassa
A middle school run by a mosque.

mullah
A Muslim teacher of law and religion.

Nakshbandia
The Sufi order that played a crucial role in Dagestan's conversion to Islam.

namus
The core of the ethical and moral code of Dagestan; its stands for support, sympathy, and the ability to give.

papakha
A tall astrakhan hat.

tamada
A toastmaster or feast leader.

tuhum
A clan comprising all relatives on the paternal side.

umra
A short pilgrimage made by Muslims.

yag'
Masculinity; the behavioral code informing Dagestani concepts of manhood, including nobility, gentleness, hard work, generosity, respect to the elderly, honor, courage, and charity toward the weak and the poor.

FOR FURTHER INFORMATION

BOOKS

Bullough, Oliver. *Let Our Fame Be Great: Journeys Among the Defiant People of the Caucasus.* New York, NY: Basic Books, 2010.

Charles River Editors. *Dagestan: The History and Legacy of Russia's Most Ethnically Diverse Republic.* Read by Colin Fluxman. Worcester, MA: Charles River Editors, 2019. Audiobook, 86 minutes.

Kennan, George. *Vagabond Life: The Caucasus Journals of George Kennan.* Seattle, WA: University of Washington Press, 2003.

King, Charles. *The Ghost of Freedom: A History of the Caucasus.* New York, NY: Oxford University Press, 2012.

Polinsky, Maria, ed. *Oxford Handbook of Languages of the Caucasus.* Oxford, UK: Oxford University Press, 2020.

WEBSITES

BBC News Country Profiles: Regions and Territories: Dagestan. https://www.bbc.com/news/world-europe-20593383.

Federation Council of the Federal Assembly of the Russian Federation: Dagestan. http://council.gov.ru/en/structure/regions/DA/.

Head of Dagestan. http://president.e-dag.ru/.

Russia Travel: The Republic of Dagestan. https://eng.russia.travel/dagestan/.

MUSIC

Ay Lazzat (Oh Pleasure): Songs and Melodies from Dagestan. Pan Records, 1995.

Sabine Kors. "Dagestan." Caspian Records, 2009.

PODCASTS

CaucasTalk. https://caucastalk.com/.

BIBLIOGRAPHY

Aleinikov, A. A., and Oksana Lipka. *Dagestan: Melting Mountains*. Translated by T. B. Shishkina. WWF-Russia, 2016. https://wwf.ru/upload/iblock/e71/dagestan_eng.pdf.

Charles River Editors. *Dagestan: The History and Legacy of Russia's Most Ethnically Diverse Republic*. Read by Colin Fluxman. Worcester, MA: Charles River Press, 2019. Audiobook, 86 minutes.

Dobaev, Igor. "Jihad in the Islamic World and the Northern Caucasus—Theory and Practice." *Central Asia and the Caucasus*, no. 1 (25) (2004): 71—78.

Editors of *Encyclopedia Britannica*. "Dagestan." *Encyclopedia Britannica*, September 11, 2015. https://www.britannica.com/place/Dagestan-republic-Russia.

Encyclopedia.com. "Dagestan." August 28, 2020. https://www.encyclopedia.com/places/commonwealth-independent-states-and-baltic-nations/cis-and-baltic-political-geography/dagestan-republic.

Kosterina, Irina. "Life and Status of Women in the North Caucasus." Heinrich Boll Stiftung, August 19, 2015. https://ru.boell.org/en/2015/08/20/life-and-status-women-north-caucasus-report-summary-survey-irina-kosterina.

Lermontov, Mikhail. "The Gift of the Terek." Translated by T. B. Shaw. In *Blackwood's Edinburgh Magazine* 54, no. 338 (December 1843): 799. Urbana, IL: Project Gutenberg. Retrieved August 11, 2020. http://www.gutenberg.org/files/25193/25193-h/25193-h.htm.

Murtuzaliev, Sergei. "Ethnopolitical Processes in the Northern Caucasus and Their Assessment by the Population." *Central Asia and the Caucasus*, no. 3 (27) (2004): 98—105.

New World Encyclopedia. "Dagestan." Retrieved August 11, 2020. https://www.newworldencyclopedia.org/entry/Dagestan.

"Quick Reference: The President of Dagestan." Retrieved August 11, 2020. http://president.e-dag.ru/home/respublika/2013-03-24-22-29-26.

Schultz, Colin. "Chechnya, Dagestan, and the North Caucasus: A Very Brief History." SmithsonianMag.com, April 19, 2013. https://www.smithsonianmag.com/smart-news/chechnya-dagestan-and-the-north-caucasus-a-very-brief-history-26714937/.

Sinelschikova, Yekaterina. "The Peoples of Dagestan: A Diverse Population Thriving in the Mountains." Russia Beyond, October 5, 2017. https://www.rbth.com/lifestyle/326327-peoples-of-dagestan-diverse-population.

Tsapieva, Olga. "Post-Soviet Socioeconomic Development in Daghestan." *Central Asia and the Caucasus*, no. 2 (8) (2001): 168—176.

Ware, Robert Bruce, Enver Kisriev, Werner Patzelt, and Ute Roericht. "Stability in the Caucasus: The Perspective from Dagestan." *Problems of Post-Communism* 50, 2 (March/April 2003).

INDEX

INDEX

144